A Life Lived and Loved, Thanks Mr. Barham

by

Barnaby Rudge

Dedication

In memory of my beloved brother Graham Rudge,
7/10/1950 to 22/3/2022,
always in our hearts X.

About the Author

The author was born during the early days of WW2 in East London, had an interesting life, from going to school with Bobby Moore, traveling the British Isles and Europe moving Household furniture and machinery, having two brothers who each saved a life, he tried, and failed, and many other escapades.

Table of Contents

Chapter 1
The Birth of Joe

Andrew leapt out of bed, blinking in the half-light, looked at his watch, and inwardly groaned, thinking of the long, hard day ahead of him. His heavily pregnant wife, Rhoda, stirred slightly and turned over, moaning in her sleep. The date was April 16th, 1911. Their three daughters were sound asleep in the cramped room next door. There was also a small living room. No kitchen, no toilet, and definitely no bathroom. Insalubrious personified.

The address was Room 111, Shrapnel Barracks (named after Lieutenant General Shrapnel, who invented the shrapnel shell), Woolwich, London. Andy, as he was known, would have agreed with you, but he would have added, 'plenty of people are much worse off'.

Now Andy was of Gloucestershire farming stock: ginger-haired, broad-shouldered, about 5' 8" tall, very friendly, loyal, and sociable. He had enlisted with The Gloucester Regiment in March 1895, at Bristol and, not long after that, transferred to The Royal Horse Artillery. Maybe it was because he came from a long line of agricultural and farming stock that he had a particular love of horses. His schedule for that day was, with others, to clear a large building behind a stable block of various items, including two gun carriages.

This was to make room for an ambulance, a brand new Straker-Squire motor ambulance van. It heralded a new age of internal combustion engines into the British military system. The ambulance was delivered the day before from a regiment in Oxfordshire. There were only a handful in the country. He left his quarters quietly, both to not disturb Rhoda but also not to wake his neighbour and best friend Bill Cox.

Bill, also known as Smiley, had only got back in the early hours from a trip to Colchester. He had left six days before with another horseman named Richard. Their detail was to take twenty pedal cycles (specially strengthened and adapted), for use by Essex and

1

Suffolk Cyclist Battalion, which became The 6th (Cyclist) Battalion, Suffolk Regiment that year. The cycles were wrapped singly in hessian, and packed into a large wagon with a tarpaulin roof for the journey. Bill had chosen his two favourite Cleveland bays, made sure that the oil lamps were full, and set off with Richard early last Monday morning.

Their route went through Rotherhithe Tunnel. Bill always smiled as he thought of the architects putting curves in the tunnel, so the horses could not see the light at the far end and bolt. Their route involved stopping each afternoon at various garrisons en route, such that they, and the animals, could rest overnight.

Before leaving the Barracks, Andy popped first into the latrine, and then the canteen, which was already buzzing with people, for a cup of tea, and two cheese rolls. He was pleased on leaving the building to note the weather was dry but with a chill in the air. A few days before, there had been a light dusting of snow. He made his way to the stable block, and said hello to his two favourite horses, muzzling his hands round their heads. His three fellow workers arrived at the same time, and they set about their job in hand.

This was to manually sort out lots of old gear in an adjoining building, including damaged hats, helmets, riding boots, jackets, etc., from the Mahdist War. An idea entered Andy's head seeing the discarded clothing. The four men were all the same rank, but Andy had been in the regiment by far the longest, so the others deferred to him. He suggested, 'Why not put the least damaged items in an old haybox? We may be able to pair undamaged shoes/boots/riding boots into pairs'. The others readily agreed, and it made a demoralising job easier.

They had been working for about four hours, and getting very hungry when a voice, shouting 'Andy, where are you '?! came from the stable block. Andy ran round the corner and was confronted by Smiley looking flustered. 'Andy! Come · quickly!' he said, very agitated. It's Rhoda – she is in a very bad way. Screaming in pain'! Andy shouted to his workmates, 'Ok lads, break for lunch! I'll meet you back here later. Get on with the job if I'm held up'!

Andy and Smiley ran back to their quarters; as they got closer to

2

Room 111, they could hear screams and raised voices. Smiley's wife Gill had taken Andy's three youngsters along with her own two, and gone down to the canteen, leaving a medical orderly with Rhoda. Slim and petite, Rhoda had given birth to three daughters without a whimper.

She looked in a terrible state: her face was bright red and distorted with pain. A nurse was holding her hand and gently wiping her heavily sweating forehead. She said to Andy, 'I have despatched a male medical orderly to run and get a wheeled stretcher; we need to get her to hospital fast'. Andy, having been involved in the field of battle, thought very fast and calmly. 'I have a plan Smiley. Will you help me'? Smiley loved and admired Andy, having been in lots of scrapes with him, and knew deep down that Andy, on the battlefield, would die for him. They had joined up on the same day and were like brothers. 'Of course mate, anything at all'!

'Good. When the stretcher comes, we'll put Rhoda on it and run her along the corridor out towards the stable block where the new ambulance is and put her inside. You hold tight to the stretcher. I know how to start the ambulance. I'll drive it the mile to the Royal Herbert Hospital. We'll run Rhoda in there; if I get court-marshalled, tough'.

Not many minutes later, they arrived at hospital, with several people milling about. They looked on open-mouthed as this strange vehicle pulled up at the main entrance. The boys reversed the procedure and had the wheeled stretcher with Rhoda now clinging on, going at a fair pace towards the examination room next to the operating theatre. A doctor appeared and ushered them into the examination room. Rhoda's face was taking on a grey sheen. He asked Andy why they were there.

Andy told him he was very concerned that Rhoda was actually in labour, and something was radically wrong. She had given birth three times before, each time relatively painlessly and quickly. The doctor motioned Andy outside the door while he examined her; he soon came out into the corridor, looking for help. Just then, Andy noticed a group of people coming along the corridor towards him. One of the group was a man in full military regalia. The doctor ran up to them and spoke hurriedly to the uniformed officer, then he and the officer walked swiftly in to the examination room, and an agonised Rhoda.

. In no time, the doctor and officer (who was now dressed in a green operating uniform) were pushing the stretcher with Rhoda into the operating theatre. They took a nurse in with them, Andy sat on a chair outside, deeply concerned at what might be the outcome. An hour went by, and suddenly Andy (who was just dozing off) was woken with a start by a baby crying.

He sat there, scared to move, for another half hour, with nurses running in and out of the theatre. Then the double doors opened, a nurse emerged carrying a baby, followed by the doctor pushing the stretcher with a sleeping Rhoda on, followed by the officer. All of them went into the examination room, and the doctor called Andy in.

The doctor said that the officer, who was The Brigade Surgeon, had been on site inspecting some improvements. The doctor, on seeing him, had called him in for advice. His diagnosis was that the baby had breached the womb, and worse, the umbilical cord was wrapped round the baby's neck, strangling it. To be sure of saving the baby's life, a Caesarean section was needed there and then.

With the Brigade surgeon taking the lead and the doctor helping, the baby's life was saved. [And my Dad had made a triumphant entrance into this world.] Andy asked the Brigade Surgeon if he could have a word, and the Surgeon said, 'Of course'. Andy explained that he had borrowed (in extreme circumstances and without permission) the brand-new ambulance. The Surgeon said, "Don't worry, I would have done the same. You saved your son's life. I will explain to your commanding officer".

Strangely, the first successful Caesarean section carried out in the British Empire was by a woman masquerading as a man (James Miranda Stuart Barry, serving as a physician in the British Army in South Africa between 1815 and 1821. Information courtesy of Wikipedia.).

Andy and Smiley took the ambulance back; the three chaps were just finishing tidying the big store area and soon-to-be ambulance garage. Andy and Smiley helped them finish off, and then the five of them had a good rummage through the discarded clothes, boots, etc., each finding several good items. Andy's best find was a top-quality dark leather left-foot riding boot, the right one cut open with a sabre. Then a perfect right foot with matching leather, the left one had two musket ball holes, a perfect end to a brilliant day.

Rhoda and the new baby were kept in hospital for six days. Andy went to collect them in the smartest wagon in the camp. They took the baby to the canteen to show him to their friends. And to meet his three sisters; their names were Ethel Winifred, Evelyn May, and Kathleen Nora. His name? Joseph Andrew Thomas Rudge. A sister, Constance Hilda Rhoda, and brother, Albert George, were to follow in the next three years.

The following year Andy, with Smiley, took part in RFA 85th SA AC Salonica Field Forces. They were both gunners, indicated by metal shoulder tithes, RFA and RHA, which meant the wearers were dressed as mounted men. An RGA tithe indicated foot soldiers; the Salonica War (21-10-1915 to 30-9-1918) was a theatre of World War I. An attempt by Allied powers to aid Serbia against the combined attack of Germany, Austria-Hungary, and Bulgaria. The boys fought well and with distinction, and both came home safe, now with prefixes Bombardier to their rank and, of course, with Bill smiling!

Chapter 2
When Joe Met Doris

Joseph Andrew Thomas Rudge, hereafter known as Joe, grew up fast at the Shrapnel Barracks, Woolwich, going with his older sisters to the local Greenhill School. He was a confident boy, quick at learning everything, excelled at swimming in the local baths, and won several medals.   He loved helping his dad Andy (who came back from The Salonica War when Joe was four) look after the horses, and could muck out a stable as well as an adult in about 20 minutes. There was an Officer on site who formed an affinity with Joe that was to last a lifetime.

This was Captain Brian Delaney, who had seen Joe many times around the stables complex. He detected a trait in Joe that was above his years: he always wanted to know how things worked, and, what made them work. Their bond was made stronger when Captain Delaney told Joe he could call him Brian, his first name. Brian was 32 years old now, and had been married to Heather, a Scots lass, for the past seven years. There were no signs of them having children. Maybe he thought of Joe as a surrogate son; he was 11 years old.

That year, 1922, Brian's mother, Caroline Delaney, passed away, and his father Sean, also an officer in the RHA was killed in action in WWI. Caroline had been living in a suburb of Dublin, in a nice Georgian house. Brian didn't want to live there as he loved London, and so the Dublin house was sold. An only child, Brian was the sole beneficiary of the sale.

With the proceeds, he bought himself and Heather a flat in a big house on Blackheath. He also bought a 1920 Triumph SD 550 cc motorbike, with a Watsonian sidecar. He loved it, as did Heather and Joe, who was becoming ever more their firm friend. The three of them could often be seen out and about on it, with Brian always driving, usually with Heather on pillion and Joe in the sidecar.
Although there were occasions when Heather would let Joe go on the pillion. She would then get in the sidecar, especially if she had

her hair coiffured.

It was around this time that Brian told Joe about Woolwich Polytechnic Technical School for Boys. Partly because he saw Joe's potential, and because he really liked him and wanted him to have a trade in life. There was an initial fee for gaining admission, which Brian offered to pay out of his recent windfall. He knew that Joe's dad, Andy's meagre army pay, with lots of mouths to feed wouldn't stretch to it. The three of them met to discuss it, and it was agreed.

On starting at the Poly, Joe found out that, aside from the three R's, there were lots of practical skills to learn. These included General Engineering, Mechanical Engineering, Carpentry, Pre-stressed Concrete, and Electrical Engineering. Andy and Brian were over the moon when Joe came home the first day and announced that he had put his name down for every course. Because of his age, he could only do two courses for the first two years, and then if he wished he could add another as an evening class. Everyone was delighted, especially knowing that Joe would want to be the best in the class at everything. Little did anyone know at the time just how useful that would be in WWII.

Joe was loving Brian's friendship and tutelage. Neither of them had told anyone, but sometimes, when the ground was dry, they would go on the combo to the far side of Woolwich common. And there, Brian would let Joe drive it, initially with Brian sitting very close behind him with arms wrapped tightly around him so that he had control of the steering, clutch, and throttle. Joe picked it up like his schoolwork – much like a sponge soaking up water. From that point on, Joe had a strong affiliation with all types of motor vehicles.

Joe's siblings were omnipresent; however, the sister immediately above him in age, Kathleen Nora, always known as Nora, was by far the closest. Nora actually said to Joe one day (bearing in mind that their mum Rhoda, was quiet and mouselike, as were the other four siblings, whereas Nora and Joe were much more outgoing like their Dad, Andy), 'Do you realise Joe, that you and I are the only Rudges, the rest are Banticks'? (Mum Rhoda's maiden name).

The years rolled by relentlessly, and Joe passed out of the Polytechnic as the top pupil. Andy, Rhoda, and all the children now lived in a dilapidated old house not far from the Barracks. Andy knew the owner, an old military man; he said to Andy one day, 'I know you and your family live in very cramped conditions. If you want, as my house is three-storey, I could move up onto the top floor, and you can use the rest of the house. No need to give me any rent – just do the house up in your own time'.

Andy jumped at the offer. The house needed various work done, some windowsills were broken, and there was no electricity, only gas lighting. A few days later, Joe said, 'Do you realise, Dad, that I can do most of the renovations on the house, including putting an electric circuit in'? Andy hadn't realised till that point how brilliant Joe's courses would turn out to be.

Joe, typical of the young man he had become, immediately got to work. Brian had said to him from the start, 'Look, I know you haven't got any tools. I want you to do some work on my flat when you finish. So, let me buy anything you need. You can pay me back later'. Obviously, Joe agreed, and then Brian remarked, 'Oh yes, I have just remembered … you know my friend Frank'? Joe nodded. 'Well, I have told him about you and the Polytechnic. He has bought a big old house on Shooters Hill Road, which is in a bit of a state. He asked me if you could do some work there. He will pay you weekly'.

Joe gave a broad smile, thinking how much his world had improved, and in a very large part because of Brian's helpful and thoughtful attitude. By the time Joe had finished his schooling, his 19th birthday was fast approaching, and he had done the work Frank needed done. Frank, like Brian, was a Captain in The Royal Horse Artillery. He had paid Joe handsomely; it was at his suggestion that Joe opened an account at the nearby Woolwich Building Society.

That summer, there was a big Fair on Woolwich Common. Brian, Frank, and their partners invited Joe along. Frank had bought a BSA motorbike and sidecar, his partner Hilary was a very jolly person, with a great sense of humour, and as Frank frequently said, 'Would laugh to see a pudding roll'. It was a glorious sunny day, the girls had made a brilliant picnic that included hand-made pork pies, cheese and pickle sandwiches, salad, sorbets, and a big currant cake with icing on top. Joe felt very happy and privileged to be in such company. The Fair was quite nearby, and he went in Frank's sidecar. The food and drink were in Brian's. They parked the combos side-by-side, with a big gap in the middle for them to have their picnic.

As they walked around, the first thing they noticed was a large, strange-looking, wooden, circular, temporary building. This turned out to be the 'Wall of Death'. Not long over from America, spectators would walk up a wooden staircase to a viewing platform to look down into the big circle which had a motorcyclist riding horizontally on the inside wall, held by centrifugal force. The force was so strong that the whole building shuddered, and, coupled with the excessive noise of the virtually non-existent exhaust system on the motorbike, made the audience gasp with excitement.

Brian and Frank were fascinated; they were both very adventurous and competitive. When the show shut for a half-hour interval, they both rushed down to see the owner and main rider, George 'Tornado' Smith, a man as eccentric as any of Britain's great eccentrics. He told them that he had a pet lioness who rode with him in a sidecar.

She wasn't there that day as the Woolwich Common Commission wouldn't allow it. Both the boys begged him to let them have a go, offering him good money for the thrill and explaining to him that they were expert horsemen and motorcyclists. Eventually, he agreed, saying, 'Ok, only ride singly. I trust you to obey my orders: no more than half throttle and no higher than two-thirds up the boards. I will take your money as no spectators will be allowed, including your wives and the young man'.

Joe and the girls stood outside; the noise really got their adrenaline going. As the riding stopped, the girls walked over to start preparing the picnic. The boys came out looking quite flushed, and Tornado complimented them on their guts and enthusiasm. Turning to Joe, he said, 'And what about you, young man? Didn't you fancy it?'. Joe just blushed and walked away, neither knowing that their paths would cross a few years later.

The picnic was voted a success by everyone, and Joe felt more than ever, comfortable and gradually getting closer to his new friends. They made their way home afterwards, and as they were saying their goodbyes, Brian said to Joe, 'Why don't you make some signs up and put them around the town saying, "Professional carpenter. General building, and electrical work undertaken', and your address"? Joe walked off with a big smile on his face; his older, wiser friend just never ceased to amaze him.

The next few months flew by. Joe had quite a few enquiries and was now officially 'self-employed', as he would be for the rest of his adventurous life, not counting his WWII Years. Christmas came and went, and the house Andy, Rhoda, and the rest of the family lived in was finished and in tip-top condition thanks to Joe's endeavours. Henry, the householder who lived on the top floor, was eternally grateful. Joe was spending quite a lot of time with his new friends, and among other things, perfecting his motorbike handling skills. Always off-road, which was easy, given the proximity of Woolwich Common.

Before he knew it, the year was over, and it was January. Another four months, and he would be 21 years old. His bank account was growing nicely, thanks to his burgeoning business, and, for the first time, he contemplated buying a motorbike. He had seen a sign in a shop window in Woolwich High Street saying, 'Rudge Ulster 500 Motorbike for sale, low mileage, may need attention as has been in my shed for two years. Unable to ride it because of a worsening war wound. Make an offer. Mr.White, 10 North Street, Woolwich'.

Joe went straight round to view it. A man, about 50 years of age, walking with the aid of a stick opened the door. Joe said, 'Hello, Mister White, my names Joe. I've come to see the motorbike you are selling'.

'Oh', said Mr. White, looking surprised. 'I only put the sign there yesterday; come to the shed, and I'll show it to you'. They walked down the garden to a particularly run-down-looking shed. Mr.White couldn't open the door; it was looking low on its hinges. In truth, it hadn't been opened for two years. Joe lifted the sagging door, and pulled hard. Strong as he was nowadays, it was still quite an effort.

After many creaking noises, it suddenly swung open. A couple of small mice scurried away as the shaft of weak wintry sunlight shone through. The bike looked in a sorry state; Mr.White had put an old piece of tarpaulin over it, but it wasn't long enough. It had protected the handlebars, fuel tank, and seat, but not the rear mudguard, which had heavy rust deposits on it.

Joe moved it slightly, both to get a better look and also to try and start it. He turned the fuel tap in line, and gave a few hefty kicks to the starter pedal after turning the choke on. It would not start, although it spluttered a few times, giving Joe the confidence to think that if he cleaned the carburettor and spark plugs, and put some new petrol in, it would definitely start. At this point, he said to Mr. White, 'What is your lowest price? Bearing in mind it is in a state and won't start'.

'Well, I paid £85 for it, brand new in 1924. I know it's in a state; I was hoping for £35'. Joe took a deep breath; he had £35 in his bank account, but didn't know how much it would cost to sort out. He said, 'I don't think you will ever sell it for that. Anyone buying it would spend a fortune repainting it and on mechanics charges. My top and final offer is £20'.

'Alright, when can you bring the cash and collect it'?

'Tomorrow morning 10 a.m., ok'? Mr.White nodded in approval.

Joe leant it back inside against the shed wall and put the bit of tarpaulin back in position. As he turned to leave, he noticed the number plate for the first time and smiled. JR 1911. Unbelievable, his initials and birth year, and on a Rudge bike, his name!

Joe knocked on Mr. White's door at 9.50 the next morning, with 20 crisp one-pound notes in his pocket. Mr.White had already written out a receipt and given it to Joe with the bike's logbook. After extricating the bike from the shed Joe noticed, not surprised, that the air in the tyres was quite low. He hadn't realised yesterday as the shed was so full. Mr.White saw him look and exclaimed, "Oh, I'm glad you noticed that. I have just remembered that there is a bag on a hook at the far end of the shed with a helmet in it. And a footpump. You can have them both with my compliments'.

Joe walked in, saw the bag, grabbed it, and walked out. He connected the foot pump, first to the front tyre, then rear, and after pumping them up, he pushed the bike onto the pavement. He shook Mr.White's hand firmly, saying, 'Thank you very much. If you get any problems, of any nature around the house, I can come and fix them, anytime, at trade price'. With that, he put the receipt and logbook in his jacket pocket, hung the bag with helmet and footpump on the handlebars, and pushed his new (to him) motorbike, the first of many, up the street towards home.

He got within about 500 yards of the house and realised that from there on was a slight downward slope. He said to himself, 'Why not'? Leaning down to turn the petrol on, he switched the ignition on and, sitting side-saddle, coasted to the house, gripping the clutch lever, slipped it into gear, and let the clutch out. The engine spluttered several times, then roared into life. He immediately grabbed the clutch lever again so that the bike didn't go roaring off and came to a controlled stop by his front gate.

His dad, Andy, happened to be walking down the path as he had a late start that day. Looking at the motorbike ticking over, albeit slightly unevenly, he let out a whoop! 'Fantastic! Boy, I am so pleased for you', and literally skipped off to work.

A few weeks later, Brian bumped into Joe by the stables; they grabbed each other and hugged, such had their relationship developed. 'Hey', said Brian, his Irish drawl slightly exaggerated as it was when he was happy and excited. 'I hear you have got yourself a super motorbike, with an Irish name to boot'.

Joe smiled back, looking slightly bemused. 'Irish? It's my name, a Rudge', at that Brian doubled up with laughter.

'Bejasus, I thought it was a Rudge Ulster me bhoy', at that they laughed again and had another, bigger, tighter hug. 'Now listen', said Brian. 'I have arranged a spiffing trip with Heather, Frank, and Hilary. We're going, in early June, and taking both our combos, up to the Isle of Man to watch the TT races, staying a few days, then coming home'!   Joe was pleased, but thinking, 'I wish I was going, maybe next year'.

Joe's birthday came and went, 22 now, he was still busy working on properties. He had just made a new friend, Jim Watts, the son of a man whose house Joe was wiring. Like Joe, he had a motorbike, also a Rudge, slightly smaller than Joe's with a 250 cc engine. They quickly became firm friends. Jim was two years older than Joe and worked as an engineer at Barking 'B' Power station. The first of June arrived, and Joe went to see his four best friends off on their trip to the Isle of Man. Brian told him they had all booked into the 'Keppel Gate Hotel' on the TT course. Brian being very methodical, had packed lots of things they probably didn't need, including his tool kit just in case, packing it all into his super Watsonian sidecar.

Their journey North West was quite uneventful, the sun was shining, and they were all in top spirits. The ferry trip was interesting, and then the island. None of them had been there before, and they were all enthralled. The hotel was very nice; everything was slotting nicely into place, and they loved the scenery, especially round the Keppel Gate.

They checked in and took their cases up to the rooms, which they were pleased to note both had balconies. The girls unpacked, each picking a nice fascinator to wear that evening, while the boys went down to the bar for a drink. As soon as the girls came down, they all had a quick aperitif and then went into the dining room for an evening meal. There was much jolliness and laughing, everyone was in great spirits especially looking forward to the first days racing tomorrow.

They were all up early next morning. Over breakfast, Brian had an idea,'Frank, I've been 'tinking'', that was his natural Irish talk coming out again. 'What about if I disconnect our sidecars? I have my toolset with me. Then this evening, after the racing has finished, you and I can have a race round the course'?

Frank thought about it for 20 seconds, then replied, 'OK, you're on! But only if we have a £10 wager on who wins'.Now that was a lot of money in those days, but both the men were quite well-off, and, as I mentioned earlier, very competitive. They hated losing.

Brian and Frank stood up and spat on their hands, before ceremoniously shaking them. The women looked on, somewhat apprehensively. Brian's Irish eyes were blazing in the way that Heather so disliked. The men went to the car park to get the toolbox to separate the bikes from the sidecars. The TT races were very exciting to watch, but each man's mind was on the night's duel – with both bursting to win.

That evening they all had an early evening meal, the atmosphere was tense, the women even tenser, their fascinators looking at times to be almost trembling. The men restricted themselves to only two glasses of wine each. Frank was not aware that when Brian went to his room afterwards to get his riding gloves, he had a really big slug of Irish whiskey from the bottle in his suitcase. The girls sat chatting at the table, waiting as the boys went out to their bikes.

They had all noticed a bench seat just along from the hotel, by a nasty left-hand bend. The boys suggested they sit there waiting to see which motorbike came along first. The boys had chosen to go round the course anticlockwise. The bench with the girls on by the hotel would be the finish line, they set off with a rolling start, the sky now with maybe just a few rainclouds. A quick nod to each other but no smiles, each over revving, they roared off.

During the first half of the course, they were neck and neck, but then Brian saw a chance to break away on a long climb. He got in front, but only by a bike's length. This carried on until, with only a mile to go, Frank pounced on a bend. It had just started raining, and the road surface was slightly slippery, probably not helped by the TT race earlier. Brian was fuming with his loss of concentration, intent on snatching victory on the last bend, the tricky left-hander.

They went into it handlebar to handlebar, each trying their damnedest. Coming out of it, Brian noticed the girls on the bench and gunned his machine forward with one last thrust causing the back end of his bike to twitch sideways, touching Frank's bike. They both momentarily lost control. Heather noticed and jumped up in fear, running towards them; Frank managed to regain control. Brian didn't.

His bike catapulted into the air, hurtling towards Heather; Hilary wasn't sure as to what hit Heather - Brian or his motorbike. A crowd hearing the noise, came running out of the hotel. One of them happened to be a Doctor. Examining Heather first and finding her unconscious, he decided that she had been struck heavily in her

15

thorax by either Brian or his bike.

He next looked at Brian and wasn't surprised. By the angle of his head to his body, he had broken his neck and was dead. Brian was taken to the mortuary, and Heather to a local cottage hospital, where due to complications – broken ribs sticking into a major blood vessel, and lungs filling with blood - she passed away during the night.

Frank and Hilary were in a state of extreme shock. The next morning, after going over the situation endlessly during the night, they decided on their next course of action. Bearing in mind where they were and the fact that neither Brian nor Heather had any living relatives. Could they possibly be buried on the Island? How soon, and where? After speaking to the hotel manager, who was most helpful, they went to a local Funeral Director. His name was Connor Flanagan, an Irishman who had been born on the Island, and whose father had started the business many years before.

When he found out that the late departed man was a Dubliner, absolutely nothing was too much trouble. He said that as the funeral trade was quiet in June, with most people dying in the winter, he could schedule it for the next day. He could make arrangements with the cemetery, and florist, and supply two hearses and a car for Frank and Hilary. He would bill them at their London address; they instantly agreed.

After leaving the Funeral Director's, they returned to the hotel to book their room for another night. Frank fitted his sidecar back on and put Brian and Heather's clothes in Brian's sidecar, along with Brian's tool box. He put Brian's house keys into Hilary's bag. Brian's sidecar was to be sent to Blackheath by train. Just as they left the Hotel, Frank asked the manager to dispose of Brian's crumpled motorbike, and send him the bill. The funeral was heartbreaking for both of them and something that affected them every waking moment for an eternity.

Their journey south was uneventful; however, they stopped in several lay-byes and gazed aimlessly at trees, valleys, railway lines - anything at all. They did not even realise what they were looking at, nor why. When they eventually got home, they decided to try and avoid Joe, who was aware that the four friends had gone to the TT races and would be home any day. Joe was excited to know how they got on.

The next day he saw Frank pulling into the Barracks on his combo and ran across to greet him and find out the news. Frank had seen him and pulled over, thinking, 'Oh God! No'! He was slowly getting off the bike as Joe ran up. Joe immediately noticed his white face, set expression, and bloodshot eyes.

Frank walked slowly round to Joe, gave him a bearhug, and burst out into uncontrollable sobbing. He couldn't talk for ages. Before he did, he insisted that Joe sit on the driver's saddle. Joe was absolutely mystified and, suddenly, extremely frightened. It took a good half hour for Frank to compose himself, and then, he blurted out, 'They're gone! They're gone! My best friends, both gone'. Frank was totally beside himself, and then while gripping his fingers and thumbs tightly, he started talking.

By the time he had finished, they were both crying floods of tears. He realised that he couldn't go to work that day. Joe said, 'Please come to my house and have a cup of tea. Mum, Dad, and the kids are all out, and we can talk in peace'. That is what happened; Joe made two cups of tea and sat down. Then Frank said, 'Some time, I have got to go to Brian's flat and see if he made a will or left any instructions'.

They decided that was what they would do together, there and then. Luckily Frank had put the key to Brian and Heather's flat onto his keyring, so he already had it with him. It felt unbelievably odd to both of them going into Brian's flat. Everything was so neat and tidy. They felt like intruders but, unfortunately, had no choice. An obvious place to look was in the beautiful old bureau.

Opening the top drawer, they saw an official-looking brown envelope. Written on it very neatly were the words, 'Only to be opened upon my death, signed, B. Delaney, dated 14.7.1928'. Frank opened it with shaking fingers. Inside the envelope was a note saying, 'If this has been opened by either you, Heather, Frank, or Joe, I want you to know that I loved you, and it was a privilege and honour to know you, God Bless', written in his neat hand.

17

On another sheet was the name of a London solicitor with an explanation. 'Ashurst, Morris, Crisp and Company, 17 Throgmorton Street, London is where my will is lodged'. They decided there and then to go to Throgmorton Street with that paperwork, especially as Frank realised he still had the death certificates in his pocket.

****

On arrival at the solicitor's office, and being asked their business, they were told to wait in a side room while Brian's will was located in one of the 'Will safes'. They were offered coffee which they accepted, and half an hour later, they were ushered into a large office. There, Mr. Crisp introduced himself and asked them to 'please be seated'. He ceremoniously opened a large brown envelope, and after clearing his throat, started reading.

'I, Brian Delaney, of 27 Brook Mansion, Common Road, Blackheath, London, hereby state that this is my last Will and Testament, made this day 14.7.1928'. (Witnessed by his Commanding officer and wife),

I Bequeath all my worldly goods to my beloved wife, Heather. If she has pre-deceased me, I Bequeath all my furniture and effects to my comrade Frank Clark. I Bequeath my property, 27 Brook Mansion, Common Road, Blackheath, London, to my friend Joseph Andrew Thomas Rudge, to whom I also Bequeath all monies from all bank accounts, plus my Triumph motorcycle and Watsonian sidecar'.

At that point, Joe fainted, landing, luckily, on a very thick pile carpet; Frank picked him up and revived him. On the way home, Frank told him that the sidecar was being sent down by train, and should arrive within five days. Joe was still trembling when Frank dropped him back home later. Joe went indoors and, over dinner, told his Mum and Dad of his enormous change of fortune. Saying that he had discussed it with Frank, and, after Frank had cleared the furniture, he would put the flat on the market.

If and when the flat sold, he would put the money in his Woolwich Building Society account until he found a good investment.   Oh, and by the way, any furniture Frank didn't want Andy could have. At this, Andy's and Rhoda's eyes really lit up; they knew it would all be top quality. Five days later, the Watsonian sidecar arrived at Woolwich Train Station. Within two hours, Joe had fitted it to his motorbike, tears running down his face as he did so.

Two days later, Joe met Jim Watts, who told him that he was going to a dance with some friends that night at East Ham Town Hall.   'Why there'? Asked Joe.

Jim replied, 'They are people I work with at Barking Power Station. The dance is good fun – why don't you come'?

'Ok, then. I'll see you there', Joe said. That night, he got ready to go out, having cleaned his new combo and put on his best clothes. Joe drove through Blackwall Tunnel, feeling a mixture of extreme sadness and, at the same time, excitement at what the future might hold. On arrival, he saw that there was a car park at the back of the building. He parked up and walked in. It was very busy, but he soon saw Jim with quite a few other people.

He walked over and got introduced to everyone. Then the band started playing, and everyone went to the dance floor. When the music stopped, people drifted back to where they had been standing. Joe was next to a couple of girls in the group. The girl nearest to him said, 'I haven't seen you here before. Do you live locally'?
'No, but not too far away at Woolwich, how about you'?
'I live at Barking', she replied.
'Oh, do you go to work'?
'Yes, I work as a seamstress for my dad, who is a tailor'.

As the next dance started, Joe found himself asking this girl if she wanted to dance with him. He had noticed that she seemed quite shy and expected her to say no, but the answer came straight back, 'Yes, please'. During the intermission, they exchanged names: Joe, and Doris.

The dance seemed to go on for ages when Doris suddenly said to Joe, 'Oh, no! My friends and I've missed the last bus'!

Joe asked, 'How many altogether'?

'Four', Doris answered.

'That's alright – I can take you all'.

Why? Have you got a car'? Doris queried.

Joe laughed, and said, 'No, but I can fit you all on my combo'. He realised then that his mate Jim had already left, probably to get up early in the morning for work. He walked out to his beloved Rudge Ulster with the gleaming sidecar, kicked it into life, and drove to the front doors. Luckily neither Doris nor her friends were very large. Joe squeezed the two smallest into the sidecar, then got Doris and another friend, Ann, to sit behind him. He told them, 'All hold very tight'! Ripple Road, Barking, was only two miles away, so the journey took no time at all.

Doris was the last one off and said, 'Thanks so much. Will you be there next week'?

Joe gave a broad smile and, revving up as he drove off, shouted, 'Definitely'!

That is truthfully how my Dad met my Mum nearly a century ago.

Chapter 3
Hitler's V2 Rocket Just Missed Us

It was noon, Sunday, 14th January 1945. I was nearly five years old and listened as the church clock struck midday for the last time ever. I was playing with my toys, while Mum's spaniel, Patsy, sat beside me in a Morrison shelter. We were in the ground floor front room of Nan and Grandpa's house in Barking, East London. It was about 70 yards from the church, and we were in the fifth year of the Second World War. Church services were still taking place, and were usually well-supported. We were all in the habit of sleeping huddled together in the Morrison shelter each night.

There had been many night-time bombing raids throughout the war. The adults were in the kitchen at the other end of the house preparing Sunday dinner. Unbeknownst to us, five minutes before, the German Wehrmacht under Adolf Hitler had fired up a V2 rocket at Loosduinen, situated in The Hague, Netherlands. The rocket's target was London. The rockets were the world's first long-range guided missiles. Their launch time was 12.01, they were 28 feet long, weighed 13 tons, and travelled 3,000 miles per hour. This was in the early days of their use, with the launch itself fraught with danger. Indeed, some of them failed to launch on the first attempt. Approximately 9,000 people were killed in the year that the V2's were used. Approximately 12,000 labourers and concentration camp prisoners died while being forced to produce the weapons.

The rockets were the first man-made missile to break the sound barrier, and were silent when travelling. Survivors only realised what had happened after the impact. Suddenly Patsy let out a strange, loud yelp/whine, and almost simultaneously, the whole house visibly shook. Every window in the house shattered, and the very heavy shelter we were sitting in moved a few inches across the floor. From the kitchen came a blood-curdling scream.

Mum came running along the passage from the kitchen, closely followed by Nan and Grandpa. Mum's face was unrecognisable; blood was pouring out of a deep gash on her forehead, running down

21

her cheeks and dripping off her chin onto the floor. After checking to see that I was uninjured, Grandpa ran back to the kitchen and came back with some hot water in a bowl, soap, a flannel, and a towel. Mum sat on an armchair for Nan and Grandpa to clean and examine her. By now, I was screaming with fear wondering what could have happened. Grandpa, as calm as ever, said, 'Don't worry, boy. It must have been a bomb landing nearby. I will go out and check as soon as I have cleaned up your mum'.

Just then came a knock on the front door; Grandpa jumped up to answer it and came back into the room with Walter Eveleigh. He was a very nice gentleman who had worked for my Dad before the war, acting as a chauffeur for weddings, etc., driving an Armstrong Siddeley car that Dad had bought for that purpose. Dad had started a household removal business and car hire facility locally in 1937. Walter had helped him with both.

Although having been invalided out of the First World War with leg injuries, he wasn't much help moving furniture. He was a first-class driver of both the lorry and car. When Dad got called up, he left Mum in charge with Walter helping her. If any local houses got bombed, Walter would take the lorry and a couple of local fifteen-year-old lads and pick up any furniture worth salvaging. He would take them to a storage unit behind Barking Town Hall. He told us that a V2 rocket had hit our local church, demolishing it, killing several people just leaving the Sunday morning service, and injuring many more.

By now, Nan and Grandpa had cleaned Mum's face up. The cut was deep, but her right eye was of much more concern. Swollen and quite bloodshot, she couldn't see out of it.

Walter said, 'There are three field ambulances there, with Doctors treating the injured'.

Grandpa asked, 'Could you take Doris to East Ham Memorial Hospital so they could maybe stitch her forehead and check her eye'?

Walter replied, 'Of course, I'll go and get the car out of the garage now'. Young as I was, I knew that I had to seize this opportunity. I (like all kids) absolutely loved my mum, and I also loved rides in the Armstrong Siddeley. Because of the war and risk at any time of air raids, these rides didn't happen very often. 'Please, Grandpa? Can I go with Mum and Uncle Walt to hospital? Please, please'?

To my amazement, Grandpa answered, 'Alright, that might be a good idea. It will get you out of the way while Nan and I start clearing away all this broken glass'.

I'm sure that even though Mum was in a lot of pain, I saw a tiny smile on her face. Within minutes there was a hoot from outside to tell us that Walter had brought the car round. Nan insisted that I put on another jumper, and a thick coat. Grandpa walked us both out to the car, me in his arms and Mum holding him tightly as she still felt groggy and faint. Walter was an excellent driver, and we purred off in the 'Harmstorm Sidney', as I called it. The seats were upholstered in brown leather, and in the middle of the rear seat was a pull-down armrest. When the armrest was down, it had a strap running across it.

This was my favourite seat – I loved sitting on it, jumping up and down on it, and holding the strap while yelling, 'Giddy up, horsey'! Twenty minutes later, we pulled up at hospital. We walked in; it was busy, with lots of walking wounded as well as stretcher cases. A nurse looked at Mum's forehead and eye, saying, 'Sit down over there, and a doctor will see to you'. We didn't seem to have waited that long before a doctor called Mum in. I went in with her.

The doctor looked at Mum's forehead and eye and said, 'I can stitch your forehead up easily, then you will need to go to Moorfields Eye Hospital. I think you have a shard of glass in your eye'. Mum looked very worried by that statement, but I think she also realised there was no choice. It had to be done. Walter was completely unfazed when she told him.

He said, 'Don't worry, Doris, the roads are fairly quiet. We can get there in about half an hour'. I was straight back on my 'giddy up horsey', and off we went to Moorfields. Sure enough, with the lack of traffic on the roads, we were soon there. This time, Walter helped Mum and me to the main entrance, and sat us both down in the reception area. He then had to go and sit in the car as the car park was full.

After a little while, a nurse came and saw Mum, noting down

what had happened. She went and told a doctor, who said that they would have to do an exploratory examination, and that I could not be present. Mum explained about the car with Walter waiting outside, and the doctor said, 'Don't worry. I will ask one of our nurses to take Brian out to the car to wait with Walter'. This time I didn't get on my 'giddy up horsey', but snuggled up on the front seat as close as I could to 'Uncle Walt', and was fast asleep in minutes.

I wasn't aware of how long Mum was, but a tapping on the window woke me up - and there was my Mum. Walter had taken the precaution of locking the door as it was now dark, in case he too fell asleep, and someone reached inside and kidnapped me. When I realised, I became frightened and started crying. Mum looked totally unlike my Mum with an eyepatch on. She said, 'Don't worry, you are just very tired. Get in the back, and I will sit and cuddle you all the way home'. I jumped into the back of the car, Mum joined me, and I was asleep again in no time – but not before hearing Mum tell Walter that she had an operation to remove the shard of glass, which was successful.

I woke up again to find that we were back home, and Grandpa was talking to Walter. 'Thanks very much, Walter! I want you to do me one more favour: my other daughter Ida heard about the rocket and phoned to see how we all were. When I told her all the events that had happened, she insisted that we all come and stay with her for a few days. While this house was straightened up. So, I want you to take us to her house please'.

Walter replied, 'No problem at all. I will help you pack now and drop you all down to Rainham. If you like, I will stay in your house to deter any burglars. Tomorrow morning I will call on Bill and Steve, who help me with any removals, and get them to help put window panes back in etc.'.

Grandpa said, 'Thanks so much, Walter. That is very much appreciated. Let's get going, as it is already late'. I was wide awake now and couldn't believe it! I loved Aunt Ida and we were going to her house, now! It seemed as though we would be staying there for a few days. It took a while getting our clothes together and bagged up. Then the next problem was fitting them, us, and Patsy into the car.

My 'giddy up horsey' armrest had to be in the upright position, and the only place that Patsy could go was on my lap. How funny! How happy!

Rainham was only six miles away, so we were there in no time. As I said, I always loved going to Aunt Ida's - it was a great big detached house that had been built just before the war, by Uncle Ted, Ida's husband. They had two children, a few years older than me, named Iris and Alan. And guess what? The house was called 'IRAL', with a lovely varnished board with that name swinging over the front door. It had a big garden with a lawn, fruit trees, and an area for growing flowers. I had never met Uncle Ted as he was away in the war, fighting for our country when I was born.

As Walter pulled up at the door, I was just so excited! My two cousins seemed just as excited about their new 'lodgers' as they came running down the path to greet their Nan and Grandpa. Auntie Doll, cousin Brian, Patsy the dog, and last but not least, Walter. We soon unloaded the car, and my cousins and I were ushered up to bed after a glass of milk. With Alan and me 'top and tailed', Aunt Ida made all the adults, including Walter, a cup of tea. Walter then left, and Aunt Ida, along with Nan and Grandpa, insisted on the full story of both hospitals.

The next morning we were all up early. Patsy was interested in the garden, so I, along with Iris and Alan, took her outside to look round. I had forgotten that Aunt Ida had six chickens, so some of us had fresh eggs for breakfast. I couldn't get over how big Auntie's garden was! Mind you, our's wasn't small.

Grandpa was a master tailor, and had a workroom upstairs at the house. In the back garden was an enormous workshop with a big cutting table plus five industrial sewing machines. Apparently, before the war, there were five seamstresses working there daily, helped by my Uncle Cecil. He was also a tailor (who was in Egypt, and involved in the war effort, at that time). The war had put a stop to that tailoring work. After a couple of days at Rainham, Grandpa phoned the house at Barking. Walter answered, saying that everything was going well. The Council had sent a man to help, and they would be finished that afternoon. Grandpa said, Excellent! Can you pick us all up at about 6 p.m.'?

Walter agreed, and duly picked us up, waiting patiently while we all said our thank yous and goodbyes. In the excitement we nearly forgot Patsy. We were just getting in the car when Grandpa heard her barking, she had somehow gotten locked out in the back garden. Her tail was wagging like mad when Alan carried her out. Grandpa was very pleased with the work that Walter and the boys had done.

Walter had found some white paint and had painted all the wainscoting, especially where any pieces of glass had grazed it. Also to Nan's pleasure and amazement, he had managed to get some blackout curtains. Nan's had been shredded by flying glass when the rocket struck. I overheard Walter telling Grandpa an amazing story the next day. When he had returned from Rainham after dropping us off, he had felt very tired, and lain down in our Morrison shelter. He fell into a deep sleep immediately.

He suspected that he heard an explosion during the evening but thought he must be dreaming. When he met Bill and Steve the next morning, Bill remarked, 'How unbelievable was that'? 'What'? Walter asked.

Bill replied, 'Another V2 hit Barking last night. I don't know yet if there were any fatalities'.

It turned out that another V2 had hit Barking at the junction of London Road and North Street without any serious injuries we heard of. In announcing the Barking disaster, the Wartime Defence Ministry was careful to play down it's severity and to say only that a rocket had landed on a church in southern England. They did not want to help the Germans refine their aim by letting them know where their rockets were landing. The Barking Advertiser's graphic account on January 20th, 1945, of the St. Paul Cathedral bombing raid, read,

'Just after the service concluded and the congregation was leaving, a bomb fell on a church which was almost completely demolished the wooden church hall beside it. Nothing remained except rubble. The priest in charge had just recited the vestry prayer in the choir vestry and was re-entering the nave when the roof and

walls collapsed with a crash. Choirboys were divesting themselves of their cassocks and surplices, and some were injured. They were immediately rushed to hospital for treatment. The priest in charge who had conducted the service and preached the sermon had a remarkable escape, for although heavy pieces of masonry had been falling all around him, he got out without a scratch. Rescue work started quickly, and altogether six bodies were retrieved; two more died after admission to hospital. Workers succeeded in saving, almost undamaged, the altar, furniture, and drapings. The altar was submerged in the debris. The name of the priest in charge is being withheld to avoid giving the Germans any clue as to the church involved'.

After V.E. day, the Bishop of Chelmsford named him the Rev. N. O. Porter. Grandpa's house gradually returned to normal; Mum had to go back to Moorfields to have her eye checked, which was, thankfully, good. I wasn't allowed to go as I had a bad cold. Her eye lost only about five percent of vision, and until the day she died (many decades later), if you looked at her eye close up, you would notice a very tiny split by her iris.

Walter occasionally took Mum and me (me on my 'giddy up horsey' seat) to Aunt Ida's, which I loved. In February, we got a letter from Dad. At the time, he was in charge of a vehicle repair unit in Breda, Holland. The letter included a little home-made birthday card for me (22nd Feb) which was brilliant. Very confusing to me, though, as the V2 came from Holland. I didn't realise till I was older that the Northern part of Holland was still in German hands at that time.

My Dad was actually stationed with a very nice Dutch family, the Dad's name was Jack van den Ring. Over the next few months, they sent Mum and me several really nice letters and presents. These included a solid silver egg cup for me with my name cut into it, a beautiful emerald necklace, bracelet, earrings, and ring for Mum, and for Dad, a gold tiepin made into a cockerel with ruby and diamond chippings. We still have the brilliant letters with funny cartoon figures on them and Mum's jewellery.

27

Unfortunately, with the passing of so many years, the other items have been lost. I do have a photo of Dad changing an engine in a military staff car in Jack's very large workshop. I think that is why Dad was billeted there: to do running repairs as and when necessary. P.S.: There can never be a silver lining to the rocket hitting the Church, but if there was, it would be: The bombsite was not built on until 1951. It thus provided me and my mates (one of them became a footballer, Bobby Moore), with a brilliant, flint-strewn playground.

Chapter 4
After the War, Dad's Safe

My fifth birthday was a quiet affair. The Second World War was ongoing, but the Allies were making increasingly important advances in Europe. As the general atmosphere got slightly more relaxed, my Aunt Ida came from Rainham by bus to visit us more often. Sometimes, she would take me home with her for a few days, which I loved. Usually, Mum would come down, in the car with Walter driving, to collect me.

On May 8th, 1945, I had slept in until about midday, which was most unusual for me. Suddenly I was woken by lots of noise coming from the kitchen. I rushed downstairs to see what was happening. Mum, Nan, and Granddad were huddled next to the wireless. I instinctively sat on Mum's lap, and pressed closely against her; I realised this was an important moment in time.

Suddenly they all, including Walter, who had just entered the room, started clapping and cheering very loudly. Mum then explained to me that the War in Europe was over! The following day Council workmen started putting bunting around all the lampposts and telegraph poles. This absolutely fascinated me, and an idea started germinating in my mind. After breakfast the following day, I walked out of the kitchen into the back garden, which I had done on many occasions. It was a nice, sunny day, and the adults would have assumed that I was going outside to see the Bantam chickens (their feathers were amazing colours).

But I had a much more exciting, adventurous idea. At the bottom of Grandpa's garden was a gate, which I was sure I would be able to unlatch and, once outside in the alley, be able to re-latch. Near the far end of Grandpa's large workshop (where up to five lady seamstresses would work, as part of his bespoke tailoring business). I spotted an empty bucket used for filling the chicken feed bins. I found that if I turned it upside down next to the gate, I could stand on it and, with a struggle, undo the latch. Then, by taking it outside the gate, reverse the process. This worked perfectly.

29

I was now in an alley that led behind the houses and came out onto a main road about 50 yards away. I knew, having walked along this road with Mum often, that there was a lamppost and telegraph pole quite near each other. I sped along and took quite a bit of the bunting off each, wrapping it round my body and legs as I did so. Now for the next part of my adventure. Nearby was a bus stop, where I had caught a bus with Mum to Aunt Ida's, when Walter was busy. Though young, five and a bit at that time, I was fairly 'with it', and thought, 'If I stood near the lady with two children who were waiting for a bus, I would be okay'.

I walked as nonchalantly as I could, and stood, quite close behind them. I knew that I wanted a No. 87 bus, and hoped the lady wanted the same one, luckily that was the first that came along, and, even better, the lady hailed it. Lots of passersby, especially ones with children were pointing and laughing at me, I took no notice and got on the bus quite close to the lady and sat near her. I think the conductor thought that I was one of her children, which was quite convenient, fare-wise.

Both the driver and conductor roared with laughter as soon they spotted me, which quite pleased me. I knew the stop to get off at and was really pleased when the lady rang the bell for the same stop , dead lucky, so far. I got off with her and her children, I recognised the side road Mum, and I would use on our way to Aunt Ida's, and set off for 'IRAL' , the name of her house were the first two letters of her children's names, Iris and Alan. I soon reached the house, couldn't reach the doorbell, so I kicked the door as hard as I could.

Within a minute, Aunt Ida opened it, saying, 'Hello Brian, you are dressed up! Where's Mum? in the car while Walter parks it '?.

'No, I came by bus on my own'. She still didn't believe me and walked out to the road, thinking that maybe Walter was turning the car round with mum still in it. As the truth dawned on her, she suddenly screamed at me, 'You naughty boy! She will be worried sick and has probably got the Police out looking for you! You must come with me to Mr.s. Ives, so I can use her phone'!

Aunt Ida, like most people in those days, didn't have a telephone and in an emergency, would use a neighbour's. Auntie insisted that I walk to Mrs Ives with her, Mum answered the phone with her voice breaking with emotion. Ida spoke, 'Hello Doris, this is Ida. I've got Brian here, the naughty little boy! Would you like to speak to him?

'Yes! Now, Brian! I have got half of Barking Police out looking for you'. Realising the enormity and stupidity of what I had done, I burst out crying and stuttered into the phone, 'Sorry, Mum. I promise that I will never do anything like this again'.

'OK, Walter is here and driving me straight down to collect you'!

Aunt Ida thanked Mrs Ives for the use of the phone, and as we left, Mrs. Ives looked at me, winked, and said, 'Well, young man, you look brilliant and have made my day'. Aunt Ida took me back into her house and gave me a glass of her homemade lemonade, some fruit from her garden, and a currant bun. Mum came in only minutes later and screamed, 'Get straight in that car, you naughty boy! No more 'giddy up horsey' seat until Dad comes home! I think Walter was smirking, both at the punishment, and the amount of bunting that I had wrapped around me.

That was the first of countless exploits, and three years later, I got a brother Phil to aid and abet me. Followed two years after by brother Grimbo. Wow! If only I had known!

A few months after the War ended, schools started reopening. There was a big old school just round the corner from us, called Westbury School. Mum duly enrolled me there in September 1945. I soon made friends with a couple of boys, John Smith, and David Browne. During our break times, we would play about with a rather beat-up leather football; it wasn't fully inflated, but it still gave us lots of pleasure. About a month after the War ended, a parcel came from Holland, addressed to Mum and me, from a family in Breda, Holland.

We later found out that Dad had been billeted with them. They owned a soap factory with a large workshop, which Dad, being a military engineer, used to repair military vehicles daily. Mum looked at the parcel, excited and mystified. She sat at the kitchen table and ripped the packaging off, with me sitting, pressed up against her. We both had eyes popping out of our heads as she finished unwrapping it. Inside, individually wrapped, was a beautiful lady's emerald necklace, bracelet, earrings, and dress ring set. Plus, a solid silver egg cup with 'Brian' etched on it, and lastly, a man's gold tiepin in the shape of a cockerel, mounted with ruby and diamond chippings.

We were both absolutely flabbergasted. Nan and Granddad, hearing Mum and I excitedly whooping, came rushing down the passage into the kitchen. We were all laughing with joy. Nan said, 'Right Brian, I am going to boil you an egg right now – never mind that you've only just had breakfast'.

Luckily it was a Saturday, so, no school. Granddad started laughing when Nan got a Bantam's egg out of the scullery cupboard and said, "Silly old Nan, the egg cup will be too big for it'. At that, we all laughed. Nan always had the last laugh, though and wedged a small screwed-up piece of newspaper into the eggcup so the egg sat nice and upright. So, that day I christened my new, super, 'Brian' egg cup.

The days flew by, and Christmas came. Mum sent Walter down to Rainham on Christmas day in the Armstrong Siddeley to collect Aunt Ida, and my cousins, Iris and Alan. Walter was to bring them back for a big family Christmas dinner. Their Dad, Uncle Ted, like my Dad, was still involved in the winding up operations after WWII. After much pleading on my part, Mum had let me go with Walter, so I got another ride on my 'giddy up horsey' seat.

Of course, on the way home, I had to give up my 'special' seat so we could all fit in. Patsy was barking like mad when we all filed back in at Granddad's house. She loved company as much as we all did. We all had a fantastic dinner, wearing party hats, and played games afterwards. Dad surprised us by phoning from his generous host's phone, just as we finished eating. He wished us a happy Christmas. He also said he was quite busy working every day, including weekends, involved with the army mopping up operation at the end of WWII. He hoped to be demobbed before my birthday, 22nd February. About a week after he had phoned, another lovely letter arrived from the Dutch family that Dad was still billeted with.

Three weeks into the new year Mum and I got the phone call we were waiting for: Dad would be home on the 19th of February!

Yippee! You won't be surprised at my excitement. But, to put it into context, I was just short of six years old and about to meet my Dad for the first time. Mum, myself, and Patsy were up very early on the 19th; I think we were all shaking with excitement.

Dad had asked Walter to pick him up at Barking Railway Station, at about 9 a.m., and was going to phone from the station on arrival. The phone rang right on time. Mum answered it, and I heard her say, 'Joe, darling! Brian and I can't wait to see you! Walter will be straight up to collect you'. Fifteen minutes later, my Dad came into my life. I had been watching out of the front room window. My heart was thumping with excitement when I saw the car pull up. He swept into the hall, scooping me up into his arms, looking resplendent in his army uniform, the cap on a jaunty angle, with his medals on display, shining in the pale February sun.

Walter was following Dad, carrying his enormous kit-bag, which intrigued me. He asked Walter to lean it against the passage wall, and he scooped Mum up as well. Was I in heaven? He squeezed us both for what seemed an eternity, with tears streaming down the faces of all three of us. Nan called out from the kitchen, down the passage, 'Welcome home, Joe! There is a steaming mug of tea on the kitchen table. Is it still one spoonful of sugar? Oh, and one for you, Walter'.

Somehow Dad carried the two of us along the narrow passage, and down the step into the kitchen. He gently put us down and proceeded to give Nan and Granddad a nice squeezy cuddle. All the while, Patsy was running round in circles, barking and yelping. What bliss! We all, except Nan, sat down at the large scrubbed wood kitchen table. While we tried to compose ourselves, at the same time asking myriad questions, Nan set about cooking six egg and bacon sandwiches in thick white bread. Rationing was still on; a large crusty loaf had been bought that morning from Fance's, the bakers just across the road.

Mum and Nan had used their ration books to buy the bacon. Each sandwich had two eggs in it, courtesy of the Bantam chickens running loose in Nan's garden. Luckily, Patsy never took any notice of them, maybe because they were there before her. We all sat, talking and laughing. After we had finished eating, Walter left us to go over to the Yard to wash down the Pantechnicon lorry, which had to be out working the next day. Time seemed to fly past. Dad wanted to know how I was getting on at school; then he suddenly jumped up, exclaiming, 'I must phone my Dad to tell him I am home safe'.

This involved phoning the barracks of the 'Royal Horse Artillery', Woolwich, where Granddad Rudge was garrisoned. The office phone there was manned 24 hours a day, and the adjacent Military Hospital was where Dad and his siblings had been born. The telephonist answered immediately and told Dad that his father was working with a young horse in the menage. She would convey the message on his return. Dad was happy with that response and, turning to the rest of us, started on his story.

When he enlisted in the Army, he was asked if he had any qualificatons. On answering, 'Several', including mechanical engineer, carpenter, electrician, and pre-stressed concrete at college, he was immediately drafted into the RASC. He was then told to make his way to their base at Buller Barracks, Aldershot, to begin training and assessment. On arrival, he was directed to the Office, where his physical fitness was found to be very good; at school, he had been a champion swimmer. He had thought ahead and taken his examination paperwork from Woolwich Polytechnic Technical School for Boys.

Dad was told to report to the stores to be measured and pick up a uniform, then make his way to No. 18 billet. This was his temporary home until further notice. He actually enjoyed his training, being informed on arrival that all personnel were trained to fight as infantry. Dad quickly formed a strong, lifelong friendship with the man in the next bunk. His name was John Spencer.

John came from Eastleigh, near Southampton. They were together throughout the War; he had lost both parents and had no living relations. He was demobbed a week after Dad, and, having no ties with his birthplace, came to live with us. I really liked him. He worked for, and with Dad. For the rest of his long life, he was always, 'Uncle John' to me.

I was pestering Dad to show me what was in his kit-bag, and

nonstop asking him about the War. At that point, Dad undid his kit-bag, saying 'Brian, I have brought you something home', reaching in, he pulled out a strange-looking metallic object. I was fascinated, 'What is it? I asked. 'It is a Dynamo torch. It had stopped working recently, I mended it, and as I was always talking about you, at the demob area, my Commanding Officer said I could bring it home for you'. Well, I felt like the 'Bees Knees' that day and cherished it for years. I believe that you can get modern versions of them nowadays'.

Dad was reluctant to talk about actual wartime experiences, although late one night in bed when he hadn't been home long, I had a raging toothache come on. I went towards Mum and Dad's bedroom, and heard them talking quietly. I heard Dad saying, 'Some of the things that happened were horrific, Doris. On more than one occasion, we saw dead Germans by the roadside, with one or two of our soldiers kneeling beside them, cutting their fingers off to remove their gold rings, and putting them in their pockets'.

On hearing that, I felt sick, and strangely, my toothache subsided. So, I crept back to bed and eventually fell into a broken sleep. When I woke in the morning and went downstairs, Mum and Dad were making breakfast. I didn't mention, ever, what I had heard. It upset and repulsed me so much that this is the first time I have ever recounted it.

We all got into a routine, me going to school, and usually Mum took me. But if Dad wasn't busy, he was pleased to walk me round. A couple of weeks after Dad came home, a very nice letter came from the Dutch family. Jack, the father, had written it and adorned it with a couple of cartoons. One of them was an empty armchair with 'Wot, no uncle Joe here to tell us stories' below it.

Many years later, after Dad had passed on, I suggested to Mum, 'How about we, being myself, wife Beryl, youngest daughter Caroline, who was nine at the time, and Mum, go over to Holland on the car ferry from Sheerness? Both for a little holiday, and to try and see the Dutch family. We had not been in contact since the letter mentioned above – approximately 38 years! Mum, who was always as 'game as a bagel', said, 'Sounds great to me'! So we duly set off, taking with us the last letter, which had their phone number on it.

Sounds stupid, doesn't it?

But that is exactly what we did. We arrived safely in Holland, and stopped in a little hotel for the first night. It conveniently had a phone booth in it (way before the 'mobile phone era'). Mum and I squeezed into the phone booth, and I, taking a deep breath, dialled the number. After a couple of rings, a man answered, speaking a language I couldn't understand. I took a deep breath and said, 'Hello, is this the family Van der Ring'?.

'Yes, can I help you'? The reply came in perfect English, to which I responded, 'I hope so. My name is Brian Rudge, my father Joseph stayed with your family toward the end of the War'.

'I see. My father has passed away; I will get my Mother. I must tell you though, that she is suffering from memory lapses'. Some time elapsed, during which I was glad that I had managed to get a good supply of Dutch coins. 'Hello', came the faltering voice of an elderly lady. She didn't sound too familiar with using the English language. 'Can I help you'?

I explained, slowly and clearly, the reason for the phone call, and she answered, 'I am sorry, but I do not remember. We had lots of English soldiers stay with us'. I, maybe for the first time in my life, did not know what to say.

I did feebly mutter, 'I am surprised that you can't remember. You cannot, surely, have sent lovely letters and expensive presents to other soldiers'? I now realise that I was hurting by the knowledge that Mum, who was privy to the call, was so bitterly disappointed. As the call ended, and I replaced the receiver, I remembered that with one of the letters was a lovely photo of Dad, with his uniform on, sitting on an armchair, surrounded by Jack Van der Ring and his three sons, which I still have.

Although the trip was fruitless and deeply disappointing, Mum and I picked ourselves up and toured Holland with the family. It included the house where Anne Frank hid from the Nazis, and was caught and killed. I am now digressing; not at all like me.

Chapter 5
My Dad

My earliest clear memory of my dad was him suggesting to me that I look after people's bikes at his garage workshop's yard. These would belong to Barking Football club supporters. The year was 1947. The football ground entrance was near Barking Town Centre, directly off the main road, Ripple Road. The workshop yard was opposite the ground's entrance; it was an open area, approximately 10 yards by 20 yards, with the vehicle workshop at one end. The entrance to the workshop had wide and high doors such that you could drive big vans through it.

Dad would work on all the mechanical parts as necessary, including changing engines/rear axles, etc. He had been in charge of a team in the War effort repairing vehicles as necessary - in both France and Holland; he was quite proficient at it. Now, in those days very few people had cars. But, quite a few - mainly men - had bicycles to get to work, their allotments, and to watch their football team. Shops surrounded the entrance to Barking Football Club, hence the idea of a 'pop up' bike park.

Dad had a friend who worked for him who, we would say nowadays, was good at multi-tasking. He made up an 'A' frame sign to stand in the yard entrance, and painted a sign on it. 'Leave your bikes here while watching the football match, 3d'. Dad's friend John Spencer (I saw him quite often, really liked him, and always called him, Uncle John) was working on a vehicle the first Saturday that we tried the 'Bike Park', experiment.

Luckily it was a dry, bright Saturday, and about 20 people left their bikes there. One man, a shady-looking person, scruffily dressed and with strong B.O., had an equally scruffy Raleigh bike. He was one of the first to arrive; one of the later arrivals had a very nice blue Rudge bike. I was admiring it, especially as my name is Rudge.

My Dad had given me a nice watch for my birthday a few weeks before, which was useful as I had an idea of the time the match was ending. And when the bike owners would return to claim their bikes.

The first man to return, just as the match was finishing was 'ragamuffin man', he went straight up to the smart Rudge bike and started wheeling it towards the yard exit. 'Hey', I shouted, 'that isn't your bike'!

At that he looked startled and said, 'Oh, yes it is'!

Luckily for me and the bike owner, Uncle John had heard the altercation and came running out of the workshop wielding the very large spanner he was using. At that, the would-be thief realised that he couldn't get away with it, and ran back with the Rudge, grabbed his own scruffy bike, and pedalled off fast. Uncle John shouted, 'And don't even think of coming back again! If you do, you'll regret it'!

Luckily, the Rudge bike owner didn't see or hear any of this, and all the bikes were collected by their rightful owners. My dad called in a while later to collect me; I told him what had happened. He thought about it for a moment and said, 'Right, come with me now to Woolworths. We will buy a book of raffle tickets. In the future, give the bike owner a ticket, and put the counterfoil on the bike to save any arguments'.

We walked round the corner (known as 'Blakes Corner', it was named after a shop bombed during the war); Woolworths was just five minutes away. Dad bought five books, and gave me the paper bag with them in it, saying, 'Take them home with you, and make sure you bring them out with you every time Barking have a home game'. We walked home together for one of Mum's super Saturday dinners.

The previous Christmas, Mum and Dad had given me a pair of roller skates. They were metal and adjustable to your feet size, with metal wheels enclosing lots of ball bearings. They had leather straps, and would fit onto ordinary shoes. I was out every day wearing them, and eventually started playing roller hockey with my mates on an exceptionally wide stretch of pavement nearby.

One day after I had been out on them for a few weeks, the front outer wheel on the left foot split open, spilling small ball bearings everywhere. My mates nearly fell over laughing at me. I managed to find a shop at East Ham, about two miles from Barking, which sold the wheels. I bought two, and a small spanner that fitted the retaining nut. I never went out on my skates again without a spare wheel and the spanner in a pocket.

On the first day of my second year of junior school, one of the new arrivals came up to the teacher's desk with his mum while I was talking to the teacher. The mum said, 'Hello, my name is Doris Moore'. At that, my ears pricked up, as my mum's name was Doris, too. 'I would like to enrol my son, Robert Frederick Chelsea Moore'.

The teacher said, 'That's fine. I see that you have filled out the application form in. You may leave him here'. Looking at me, she asked, 'Brian, would you kindly show Robert round the school'? I must explain at this point that, because of the war, there was a teacher shortage. And although my friends and I were second year, it sometimes happened that an underage pupil joined us.

Anyway, Robert and I walked off with him saying, 'Hello Brian, Mum and Dad call me Bobby, and I would like you and your mates to as well'. The next day Doris dropped Bobby off as my mates, and I were milling about in the playground playing a game we called 'Fives'. This involved several of us, in turn kicking a ball against a small section of wall until one of us missed, losing a life, starting with five lives, the last one alive was the winner.

Bobby, naturally, wanted to join in; we all said fine. I noticed that every time it was Bobby's turn to kick the ball against the wall, he would toe punt it, and invariably it would go wide, missing the wall and losing him a life. Now, I like to think that I am a fair-minded person and wanted him to have as good a chance as any of us. I said, 'Bobby, try and stroke the ball as hard as you can with your instep; it will give you more control and better direction'. My mates weren't very impressed, as it immediately improved his game and made them all try harder not to be first out, especially against a new boy!

Many years later, watching England in the 1966 World cup final, I couldn't help smiling to myself and thinking, 'Maybe, just maybe, my advice all those years before germinated a seed in Bobby's mind', ha, ha. Life was so good in those days: no more worrying about air raid warning sirens going off and running home to get in the Morrison shelter. No more worrying about Dad's safety in some far-off, 'theatre of war'. Even now, in my early 80s, if I hear something remotely like a siren, I feel a shudder go down my spine.

The following Saturday, Barking were playing at home, and it was the second trial of my minding cycle in the garage yard. I put the sign at the entrance, had my raffle tickets in my pocket, and waited for the first arrivals. The first one was the owner of the nice blue Rudge. He had heard somehow about his bike nearly being stolen and was pleased with our new, albeit simple, security system. I tore both sections of ticket No. 1 off, giving one to him and attaching the other securely behind the brake cable just below the handlebars. I was interested and quite pleased when I issued the last ticket to see that it was No. 40. This was twice as many as the first week.

Time seemed to fly, and the bike owners began streaming back, talking and smiling at each other. It turned out that Barking had won, 3 - 0. I was just putting the sign back in the garage when a tall man wearing a tracksuit came into the yard. He walked over to me; I could see a quizzical look on his face. He said, 'Hello, young man, are you in charge'?

'Yes', I replied.

He gave me a big smile and exclaimed, 'Well done, what you are doing is a brilliant idea! We are seeing new supporters now that they can leave their bikes safe. Starting with our next home game, we are giving you two complimentary tickets each time we have a home game as a thank you'. As you can imagine, my heart was racing with excitement and pleasure, 'Thank you so much, that's brilliant'. At that, the track-suited man went to walk off.

'Hold it'! I said, thinking quickly, 'If you come to the home games on your bike, you can leave it here free of charge'.

'Thanks, I may well do that'! Then he strode off smiling about it.

Dinner was on the table; I washed my hands quickly and sat down between Mum and Dad. After a few minutes, Dad said, 'Well, how did it go today'?

I had been waiting excitedly for one of them to ask. 'Absolutely brilliant', I replied, relating the day's events. Dad was most impressed, and Mum smiled happily.

Dad said, 'It's a shame, I wouldn't be able to come with you to watch any matches. You know I always play snooker in the Liberal club with Uncle Harry on Saturday afternoons'.

I laughed and said, 'Don't be silly. How could I go anyway, when I have my business to run? Guarding all the bicycles'? Mum and Dad laughed heartily at my statement.

Dad said, 'No, boy, you're the worker. I'm the boss'.

'Yes, for now', I cheekily replied.

Mum said, 'Come on, you two, eat your dinners before they get cold'.

After dinner, Dad and I sat together, talking on the settee. I said, 'I have had an idea about the two complimentary tickets'.

'Oh, yes? What is that'? Dad asked.

I said, 'Well, you know I've told you about my new friend Bobby Moore? I think that he and his Dad are very interested in football. Would you mind if I offered them the tickets'?

'Not at all. I think that's a good idea'.

Monday morning, I took the complimentary tickets to school to give to Bobby's mum. As luck would have it, his mum was ill, and his dad brought Bobby to school. I had been looking out for Bobby to arrive, so I went to straightaway to give them the tickets, explaining how they had come about.

They were both quite pleased and excited and said they would definitely use them. This really pleased me. His dad seemed a very nice man. They both turned up at the next home game. His dad was full of smiles, and, luckily, Barking won again. Incidentally, the man who tried to steal the nice bike never turned up again. I was a bike minder for three years and loved it.

Chapter 6
The Births of Philip, and Barnaby

During March 1948, my life was going along quite nicely. On alternate Saturdays, I was busy looking after the football supporter's bikes, at Dad's Garage opposite the football ground, in the middle of Barking. Gradually, more bike owners were entrusting their bikes to me, but this particular Saturday, I had something on my mind. I had woken early and walked along the landing to Mum's and Dad's bedroom. As I approached their door, I heard them talking with muffled voices. Mum said, 'I am almost certain that I am pregnant, Joe'.

I didn't know the word, but by the tone of her voice, thought it must be important and not meant for my ears, so I scuttled quickly and quietly back to my bedroom. I crept back into bed, waiting till I heard them rise. I was just slipping back to sleep when I heard Dad walking along the landing. I jumped up quickly as he opened my door, scooping me up in his arms and giving me one of his lovely squeezes. Mum joined us, and we had a group cuddle. Gorgeous! Nan and Granddad were already in the kitchen, and we all had a little natter. Granddad said to me, 'Are Barking playing at home today?'

'Yes, Grandpa. I am hoping to break my record today and get 60 bikes, at least'. At that, we all laughed. I hadn't called him that before, and he seemed to like it.

Just then, Nan said with a smile on her face, 'I suppose you'll be calling me Grandma next'.

'No', I replied. 'You'll always be Nan to me, and the only one I've got'. I noticed a tear run down Dad's face then, as his Mum had died a few years before. I had never met her and had only met Dad's father a few times. He lived with one of Dad's sisters in South London. Nan and Grandpa had met in Newark, Lincolnshire. Grandpa's father was a tailor, and Grandpa had followed him into the same profession. After marrying, they decided to move to the London area and start a family there. For some reason, they picked on Barking, Essex. Five children followed, of which my mum was the youngest. She had two sisters and two brothers. Grandpa's business burgeoned quite fast as people realised what an expert, competitively-priced tailor he was.

Nan was quite a big lady, only just over five feet tall, but weighed about sixteen stone. She had two sisters, my great-aunts, who were literally well over twenty stone, each. Aunt Ada and Aunt Alice lived in a bungalow right next to the beach at Greatstone, Kent. It had fabulous, long, high sand dunes, which you could virtually ski down. I would often stay with them for weeks on end during the summer holidays, always coming back with tar on my soles, through running about barefoot. Aaah! Memories. Grandpa, by comparison was only 5 feet 3 inches tall, and about seven stone dripping wet. 'Come on Brian, as you are working today, little man, would you like two Bantam's eggs on toast and a cup of tea'?

'Yes, please, Nan. I would love that! Shall I go out in the back garden and collect any eggs I find'?

'Yes, please. Thank you'. Nan and Grandpa had eight Bantam chickens in the back garden, all hens with lovely coloured feathers. In the garden, there was also a very large wooden workshop where up to five ladies would work on industrial sewing machines. It was part of Grandpa and his son, Uncle Cecil's, tailoring business. Grandpa was a master tailor, and the Governor of Gibraltar was among his clients, as well as one or two politicians and some officials at Barking and East Ham Town Halls.

Uncle Cecil (who was my favourite Uncle) lived with his wife Em and daughter Celia on the road adjacent to us. You could walk to their house from an alley at the bottom of our garden. I have said, over the years, that I actually felt grown up, at age seven when I was allowed to cross the main road outside the house. This was to buy rolls and cakes in 'Fances', the bakers opposite, for the lady machinists. In winter, the machinists had two paraffin heaters in the shed/workshop on continually. We would put the rolls on top of them to warm up. You might think that would taint them with a paraffin taste, but it didn't - not one bit. Oh dear, I'm digressing again.

I thoroughly enjoyed my breakfast and set off for the garage to get it ready for the football spectators and bikes. I had totally forgotten hearing Mum and Dad's conversation in bed this morning. It was a bright sunny day, and a few of my customers arrived early to get a bit of shopping done before the game. Each gave me a copper or two extra as a treat. When all the owners and bikes had arrived, I counted them, and yes! I had a new record of 64 bikes. A few weeks later, it was the last game of the season.

Mum said she would walk up to the town with me, as she wanted to do some shopping; the main shops were only about a hundred yards further. I cleaned up the yard, ready for the bikes, and realised I was low on the numbered tickets Dad had wisely suggested I use. Woolworths, where we got them, was just round the corner, so I walked there to get some more. The Town Centre was very busy. As I walked past 'Marks and Sparks', a jokey term for Marks and Spencers, a couple of people bumped into each other by the entrance doors.

A bag fell onto the pavement, right at my feet, I scooped it up as it landed, and someone tapped me on the shoulder. I looked round, and saw, to my surprise, it was my Mum, looking embarrassed. 'That's my bag Brian. I have bought myself a couple of dresses in the sale'. Now, for my Mum to shop for clothes for herself was unusual - bearing in mind that the austerity of the war years was still at the forefront of most people's minds - especially my Mum's.

I gave her a peck on her cheek, 'Good for you, Mum! You deserve it! I am just going to buy some more raffle tickets so that I can identify the bikes. Must rush - they will be arriving soon'! Giving her a peck on her cheek, off I went. I got back to the garage just in time for all my regulars. I was now averaging 60 bikes a game.

Uncle John had suggested putting an extra 'A' board out, saying, 'Bikes cleaned and oiled, including tyre pressures checked, and pumped up as necessary, 6p per bike'. Dad and I thought it was a good idea, I had my new 'A' board in place, a brush and light oil to clean the wheels and spokes, and a cleaning and polishing rag for the frame in hand. Also within reach, I had a bike pump that Uncle John had refurbished. Wearing a pair of bespoke overalls that Uncle Cecil had made me, I looked and felt the part.

Only five people wanted my 'Bike check and spruce up' that first day, but I was pleased to go home with half a crown extra. I rushed home to tell everyone the news. As soon as I got in the door, I told them all about it. I sat down for a cup of tea, and Mum came and sat beside me. I've got something to tell you, Brian. You know you saw me coming out of Marks and Spencer's today'?

'Yes, Mum'? 'Well, I'm pregnant, and my tummy is getting bigger. So I had to get a couple of bigger dresses'. There was a noticeable silence at that point. Nan and Granddad, came into the room, closely followed by Dad. 'That's fantastic, Mum! So, I'm going to have a baby brother or sister'? 'Yes, Brian, and we won't know until it pops out, which it will be'.

'Do you know when, Mum'?

'Not exactly, but it looks like it will be late November or early December'. 'That's good, Mum! Before Christmas'! At that, everyone clapped really loudly. I wouldn't say the months flew by, but it seemed like it.

I had been born at home, during the War, and the adults were expecting the new baby to be, as well. One day in early June, Nan told me, 'I am going out with my friends from the British Legion Club next Tuesday. There is a seat spare on the coach. Would you like to come? It's quite good fun'.

'I would love to, Nan! I am sure they won't mind at School'.

Mum made sure I was washed, dressed, and had my breakfast by 8.30 on Tuesday morning. My lovely Nan and I walked round the corner to the Legion, as we called it, and were the first ones there. The coach arrived 15 minutes later, by which time a crowd of O.A.P.s, were waiting. Nan had told me the usual seating system, so I sat next to her in the fourth row. The atmosphere was brilliant - everyone talking at once, with lots of laughter, mainly ladies. Yes - they had outlived the men – as now.

The main lady, called Vera, said, over a little loudspeaker, 'Good morning, everyone! We will be stopping at our favourite cafe at Hawkhurst for early lunch. Then on to Hastings for a few hours. I will now put some of our favourite songs on for you'. The songs were brilliant, some sea shanties, the old folks joined in often, the one that was the most loved went 'Bobbin up and down like this' with various verses, everyone whilst singing it would be bobbing up and down on their seats - hilarious!

We got to the cafe, and everyone alighted from the coach. Nan wanted to show me a well in the garden, so we walked down to it with some of the other old folk. There was a sign on the rocks surrounding the well, 'Can you see the water Otter'? You had to really peer down the well to see it: an old kettle, haha. I love telling people the coach story, even to this day. What a fantastic day out with my Nan and her cronies!

The next day, after school, I was out with my friends on my skates, boring them with that story. In no time, or so it seemed, autumn came, and the nights started closing in. Early November, Grandpa called me to one side, 'Brian, I have had an idea. I want to treat your Mum; she doesn't know yet, but Nan and I are going to buy her a nice pram for the baby. Next Saturday, Nan and I are going up to London by train. A big store has asked me if I could supply them with men's suits. We would like you to come with us. While there, we are going to look at prams; would you like to come'?

'Grandpa, that sounds brilliant! I would love to come with you both'!

'Good! But please don't mention the pram to Mum or Dad'.

'I promise that I won't mention a thing - and thanks again for taking me'! Grandpa had set his alarm for 6.30, saying, 'We'll have a hearty breakfast to set us up for the day'. Dad offered to take us to the Station, but Grandpa said, 'No thanks. The walk will be good for us; It's a nice bright day'.

Grandpa put some photos of recent bespoke men's suits he had made into Nan's cavernous handbag. After breakfast, we set off on our little adventure. Fifteen minutes later, we walked into the station entrance, right past W.H.Smiths' papershop. Little did I know that I was to enrol there as a paperboy on my 14th birthday.

Grandpa bought two adult, and one child return tickets to Holborn. It was still only 8 a.m. - how exciting! It was only the second time that I had been on a train; I asked Grandpa where we were actually going.

'"Gamages of Holborn", a very large, very old department store, they sell virtually everything there, they will probably have Christmas decorations already up'.

The journey didn't seem to take very long at all, we left the station, a few minutes walk, and we were there, it was by far the biggest shop I had ever seen. From the outside, it actually looked like several shops cobbled together, a bit higgledy-piggledy, enormous, and very interesting, which I really liked. Grandpa asked a member of staff where the Men's Outfitters Department was.

He was told to take a lift to the fourth floor, turn right out of the lift, and it started there. We did as instructed, and then Grandpa asked where the Manager was. We were directed to an office with windows on all four sides, an ornate door, and a very smart man sitting at a Victorian desk.

Grandpa tapped on the door, and the Manager rose sharply, opened the door, and ushered the three of us in, saying, 'My name is John Webb. Would you like tea or coffee? And what can I do for you'? There were two smart office chairs he waved us towards. Grandpa helped Nan to be seated and, lifting me up as he sat, put me onto his lap.

Grandpa smiled and said, 'Good morning, my name is William Richards. Three teas would be very nice, thank you. I am a bespoke tailor and have been in the business all my life'.

John Webb discreetly picked up an internal phone and ordered, 'Four teas, one of them milky, please, Jean'. 'Sorry about that, William. You were saying'?

'Yes, John. I believe that someone I have made suits for recommended me to your stock buyer'.

'Well, William, we do sell suits off the peg. However, our more well-to-do customers only want 'made to measure'.

'The thing is, John, that I am meticulous with my measuring and trial fittings, often basting two or three times. An example is the Town Councillor at Barking, who has a deformed shoulder. If I were to make suits for your customers, it would be very difficult unless they visit me in Barking on more than one occasion.

'Yes, I see William. I don't actually think we could make it into a viable business agreement. I am sorry about that'. At that point, Jean, from the office catering department, arrived with our teas and some delicious chocolate biscuits. Grandpa smiled and said, 'Never mind, I didn't think it could. But, I wanted to speak first-hand to one of your team'.

We very much enjoyed our tea and biscuits. (The best biscuits I had ever tasted, there were four, Grandpa said that as I was a growing lad, I could have two).

As we left John's office, Grandpa asked for directions for the pram department, 'Go down in the lift to the second floor, then look for the "Perambulators" sign'. While in the lift, we laughed again at the posh name. As we left the lift, we saw a sign with 'Tea Rooms' on it. Grandpa said, 'Let's go in there, Harriet and have a sandwich. We have earned one with all this travelling and talking'.

'Yes, please, William'. Thinking back, all those years ago, it really was a different age. For example, Nan and Grandpa used their full Christian names. We had a lovely sandwich each; they were very nice indeed. Grandpa said, 'After this, we will have a good look at the prams. I mean "perambulators"'. We all laughed and walked out the door.

On reaching the Perambulator Department, I think our eyes opened wide. They were all 'Silver Cross prams', with signs saying, 'Aluminium body, High gloss finish, Spoked wheels'. Gorgeous colours. One of the saleswomen spotted us, came straight over, and spoke to Nan and Grandpa for ages. I got the impression that it was an adults-only conversation, and just walked around on my own.

After a while, the saleswoman walked through a door at the back of the area, and re-appeared a couple of minutes later, pushing a purple pram - or 'perambulator'. Nan and Grandpa gave it a good looking over, talked together to one side, then walked over to the saleswoman again, and both shook her hand. Grandpa took, what looked like lots of paper money out of his inside jacket pocket, and gave it to the saleswoman. She handed him a piece of paper, and then Nan and Grandpa walked over to me.

'I am really pleased to have bought the pram, especially that colour. Purple has always been my favourite colour, and the price was discounted as other people didn't seem to like the colour'.

'They are going to wrap the pram up, really well, so that we can take it back with us today, so, we will make our way to the station to travel before the trains get busy'. Twenty minutes later, we were walking out of the store with our superb purchase. The only parts of the pram not wrapped were the wheels. When it arrived ten minutes later, I helped Grandpa carry the pram down the steps to the platform and onto the train.

There was no one in the carriage we got into. Grandpa put the pram brake on, and sat holding the pram so that even if the train stopped suddenly, it wouldn't move. Forty minutes later, we alighted the train at Barking Station. As we walked down Station Hill towards where we lived, Grandpa said, speaking quietly. 'Now Brian, I want you to keep a secret: we are not going straight home, but going round to Uncle Cecil's house (it was the next turning to us) to leave the pram there. Aunty Em (Cecil's wife) will be in; we are leaving the pram there until the baby is born. Then I will collect it as a surprise'.

Well, did I feel proud and privileged! I had never been privy to an adult secret before. 'Also', Grandpa continued. 'I will explain the reason that purple is my favourite colour. It was one of Queen Alexandra's favourite colours, which she wore after the passing of Queen Victoria'. I have always assumed that, Grandpa being in the tailoring business, most likely had an appreciative attitude to design and colour.

We successfully ensconced the new super-duper pram at Uncle Cecil and Auntie Em's, and made our way home (only about 300 yards away). As we walked that short distance, I thought to myself, 'Is purple a girl's colour? Is Mum going to have a girl? And, am I the only one in the family who doesn't know? Is that why Grandpa has bought a girlie-coloured pram'?

The following day Dad, who had been out doing a house move for a very good friend of his, came into the house with a big grin on his face. It turned out that the friend, Harry Philipps - who was actually my Godfather and had an electrical appliance shop – had moved out of a nice part of Barking to Loughton, an upmarket town about 10 miles away.

He was quite well off and wasn't worried about selling the house in Barking. He had said to Dad, 'Why don't you move into 11 Sandringham Road'? It was the very house that he had moved out of that morning. 'You can have it for a peppercorn rent initially, and if you want to buy it in the future, we can sort that out then'.

Dad and Mum discussed it that day, and decided to move out of Nan and Grandpa's. And did so the following day. Quite a big thing came out of it for me. I had to change schools, which was exciting for me. It involved meeting the best schoolteacher in the world. But, more on that later.

Within two days, we moved out of Nan and Grandpa's, which was sad, but only about three-quarters of a mile away. It was decided that I would stay at Westbury School till Christmas, and join Manor Junior School in the new year. About two weeks later, on Tuesday, 23rd November, I was awoken by Mum moaning in her bedroom.

I jumped out of bed and ran the short distance to Mum's and Dad's bedroom. They both looked quite concerned. I had been birthed quite easily by Mum, with Nan helping in a Morrison shelter. That was in Nan and Grandpa's front room during the early days of WW2. This was a different scenario: they said the umbilical cord might be wrapped around the baby's neck. Mum was in a lot of pain and making a mixture of whimpering and moaning noises which really frightened me.

Suddenly Dad said, 'That's it, Doris. Let's get your dressing gown on you, and get you to the hospital'. It was fortunately only about 300 yards away. 'Brian, you're a big boy now. While I take Mum, have a quick wash, get dressed and have your breakfast. They won't want me at the hospital. I'll leave Mum there and come back for you. Then drop you to school'.

Through tears, I blurted, 'Oay, Dad. Good luck, Mum'! And then rushed to the bathroom. Thirty minutes later, with tears running down my face, I saw Dad pull up while looking out of the window, and ran to the door.

He beckoned me to shut the front door and get in the car. He dropped me at my school, and as I got out of the car he kissed me and squeezed my hand, saying, ' Don't worry, boy. After school, walk round to Nan's, and I will pick you up there'. I left school with some trepidation, and walked very slowly to Nan's. The front door was always unlocked, the house being a business premises.

As I entered the hall, I could hear a strange noise coming from the kitchen which was quite a way off. It came from along a passage with a step-down, just before the kitchen. The nearer I got to the kitchen, I thought that I could make out Dad's voice, Nan's, and Grandpa's voices.

I also heard Uncle John's voice, plus maybe a high-pitched voice in the background. I hurried along the passage to find out what was happening. Pushing the door open, I saw all the faces to match the voices. Also, to my amazement, in the far corner, on Grandpa's wooden carver chair, was my mum with a large white blanket on her lap.

You could just make out in the folds near her upper arm a tiny, wrinkled, pink face topped with gorgeous blonde curls. I had never seen such a young, beautiful face before. Everyone was watching my spellbound face, 'I've got a beautiful little baby sister'!

At this, everyone burst out laughing. Dad shushed everyone, then looked at me, saying, 'It's a boy, Brian. We have named him Philip. You can give him a little kiss on the forehead if you want to'. That is exactly what I did!

Neither I nor anyone watching could have imagined that this little baby would, one day, be given a bravery award by the High Sheriff of London, for saving a man's life in the face of extreme danger.

Mum, Dad, Nan, Grandpa, little Philip, and I met up at Nan and Grandpa's on Saturday, four days later, for a 'Celebration Lunch'. We were all sitting in the front room afterwards, talking and laughing, when Grandpa got up and walked into the next room, which was essentially an office.

The rest of us stayed in the front room talking; after a few minutes, we could hear soft scuffling noises from the hall. Nobody took any notice, and then Grandpa called out, 'All shut your eyes, please'. We immediately did that and could hear from the slight sounds that Grandpa made, that he was bringing something into the room. 'Open your eyes', he shouted. Of course, we did, and there, right next to us, was the fantastic, Purple Pram.

Mum immediately burst out crying with pleasure and surprise. Even Dad, who was rarely nonplussed, let out a gasp. Nan suddenly started clapping loudly, and everyone else followed. I was really pleased that Mum and Dad loved it. Although it was late November, it was a nice sunny day, and the rays of sunshine coming through the windows really made it's purple coachwork shine. The pram was used every day; Mum's friends and even strangers stopped her in the street to admire it.

Christmas came and went, Barking Football Club had a big game on New Year's Day, and I had the most amount of bikes ever to look after. When Barking were playing at home, Mum would often walk from the Leftley estate, where Harry Phillip's house was, to see me. And do a bit of shopping, which she put in the handy pannier under the frame.

The year was now 1949. I loved my new school in which the English teacher, Mr. Barham, was nice and seemed to like me for some reason. Within a few days of my joining, he gave me the nickname 'Barnaby', which has stuck with me for well over 70 years. He, as part of his job, would put plays on the stage in the large Assembly Hall. The first one he put on after my arrival at the school was 'Robin Hood'.

I was dumbfounded when I was cast as Little John; it went off ok. And I loved his English lessons. A few weeks later, he informed the class that the next play was going to be, 'The Merchant of Venice'. We all looked at each other and smiled. He promptly wiped the smile off my face when he told me that I was going to be Shylock, a heartless, greedy, Jewish moneylender. I had to wear a wig and tattered old clothing while holding a stone and sharpening a penknife on it. Great fun.To this day, people, on hearing that, say, 'You were so typecast', ha ha.

My baby brother Philip was getting on well, and despite my pleadings to take him out in his superb purple pram, Mum was adamant that I was too young. On a bright, sunny day during my summer holiday from school, when Philip was about 10 months old, Dad was putting a shed up in the garden. He needed Mum to help him put a roof section up.

Philip was crying a lot; Mum said he was teething. She asked that if I was very careful, would I take him for a walk to the park? There were no major roads to cross, and I was told, 'Brian, you must watch your little brother at all times, do you understand'?

'Of course, Mum, I will'.

'You have got your watch on, be back in an hour and a half at the latest'.

'I will Mum'. I set off, pushing the pram very gingerly, making sure the wheels didn't go down any wide cracks in the paving slabs. Philip seemed to realise that I, his proud, big brother, was taking him out for the first time. Within about 15 minutes, we had walked through the ornate wrought iron gateway. About 50 yards on the left was the end of the line on the miniature railway. Several parents and children were milling about, waiting for the train to arrive and take them to a very large lake, a few hundred yards down the line.

I pushed Philip down the road towards the lake. Lots of people, especially mums, were admiring the beautiful purple pram; it was really shining with the sun on it, with the hood up, of course. We soon got to the lake, on which was a miniature version of a Mississippi steamboat. There were also rowing boats and sailing dinghies for hire. I walked along the footpath perimeter for about 200 yards, and suddenly spotted my friend Keith Tully; he had a rod with a net on and was fishing.

As I got close to him, I saw a large jar beside him with several sticklebacks in it. This was quite fascinating; I stopped to speak to him, leaving the pram unattended. In my excitement, I didn't put the pram brake on, nor did I notice the slight incline towards the lake. Keith seemed pleased to see me, and showed me his fish. I was kneeling down for a better look when a lady shouted out, 'Watch that pram'!

I was still admiring the fish when I heard a loud splash. I quickly looked towards Philip and the pram, and shouted, "Oh my God! The pram has gone'! My heart was in my mouth; I turned and looked now towards the lake. The pram, with Philip in, was quickly drifting outwards and, worse still, taking in lots of water, which was now level with his chest.

I was petrified; my heart felt as though it was coming through my chest, beating so hard and fast. Suddenly there was another splash; a brave, quick-thinking man had jumped in, fully clothed and was striking out towards Philip. My baby brother was screaming, with his mouth very close to the waterline, in his pram. Pandemonium broke out among the crowd; I heard that a man had sprinted to the boat office, where there was a phone, to contact an ambulance and the police.

A voice in the crowd said to me, 'I recognise you from the bike storage place by the football pitch, you're Joe Rudge's son. I've got his phone number in my pocket diary'. With that, he ran off towards the boat office, presumably to phone Dad. Suddenly, a shout went up from the crowd, 'Hooray'!!

I looked towards Philip, the pram, and the man who had jumped into the lake. He had reached the pram, just as the water waves were lapping around Philip's mouth. He was swallowing some of the murky water, coughing, crying, and regurgitating foul-looking gunge, all at the same time.

I was, for the first time in my life shaking with fear and trepidation. Would my beloved little brother live? Would I get sent to prison? Would Dad kill me? Suddenly, the crowd cheered, I looked round towards the lake. The man had Philip across his shoulder and was dragging the pram with his other hand towards the path we were all standing on. As he got to the lakeside, several men reached out to grab Philip, and others the pram.

One lady, who was quite plump, took Philip, saying that she was a trained nurse, held him upside down, and patted his back; water, weed and sick were coming out of his mouth. Just then, an ambulance, it's siren blaring, came into view, followed by a police car, in the back of which were my Mum and Dad.

The two ambulance staff rushed up and took Philip, immediately giving him attention. I was quaking when Mum and Dad got out of the police car and made straight for me. Mum was wailing her eyes out, and Dad had a very serious look on his face. He never hit me then or any other time I crossed the line in my life (and there have been a few). He just told me how stupid I had been putting my little defenceless brother's life at risk.

Maybe it was his army training, but, he never hit me or my, eventually, two brothers. Ever. Mum was beside herself; she was allowed to sit in the back of the Ambulance, with Philip in a cot next to her. It was on a trip to hospital, to get Philip checked out properly. Dad said that he and I would walk the sodden but still beautiful purple pram home. Then, once it was dry, I had to clean and polish it thoroughly.

That is exactly how it happened all those years ago. Thank God, Philip is alive and well, 73 years later, and a gifted craftsman. Oh, and another thing. I was NEVER asked to take either of my little brothers out until they were adults. Then we got into scrapes often.

Chapter 7
My Beloved Auntie Eva

My beloved Auntie Eva Gray lived in Wooler Street, Walworth, South London. She was Mum's elder sister and had three children, all older than me. She was divorced, and it was a struggle bringing up the children up on her own. Her husband, a policeman, was a bit of a bastard and very mean. My Mum and Dad would visit her, usually on a Sunday, when Dad wasn't busy.

Of course, I would go with them; later, when my two brothers arrived, they came, as well. When we visited her, she would open her front door with a beaming smile, welcome us into her parlour, and put the kettle on, saying, 'Who wants some of my "Killmequicks"'?

That was her joke term for her homemade cakes and jam tarts. She was about 5' 2" tall, quite plump, with a gorgeous smile. A very jolly woman, she had nothing, but if 'she could', would give you the Earth. She absolutely had what is known as 'a heart of gold'.

I can remember when I was eight, in 1948, her eldest child, a boy named Dennis, was getting married to Mavis in Mansfield, Derbyshire. They had met at work at Boots Pharmaceuticals' main offices in Nottingham. Dennis was an accountant at Boots, and Mavis worked in the same office. At the time, my Dad owned a 27-seater Bedford coach and took lots of family members, including Auntie Eva, my Mum, two little brothers, and me, to the wedding.

A few years ago, at a distant family member's funeral in Poole, Dorset, I got talking to Dennis's son Stephen (Dennis had unfortunately long passed), who asked if my brother Graham and I were interested in Rugby Union. We both replied in the affirmative, to which Stephen said, 'Good, I have found out today that my son, Joe Gray, has just signed to play for Harlequins Rugby Club'. Graham was most impressed as they are his favourite team. Oops ... sorry, I am digressing again.

Once, when I was ten years old, I was allowed to go and stay with Auntie Eva on my own. I still think of it in wonderment 72 years on. She would take me to East Street Market, a very famous market just round the corner from her, which was always buzzing. My Dad had given me some pocket money, so I could buy Auntie and myself a hot dog and a cup of tea, each. It was February, just after my birthday, quite cold, and there was a man with a brazier roasting chestnuts.

I hadn't seen that before and was very pleased to be able to buy us both some. We took them back to Auntie's, talked, and laughed while shelling them. Mind you, she nearly told me off for dropping bits on the floor. Aah, she always indulged me. The next morning over breakfast, I asked if I could go out exploring on my own; she thought about it for what seemed like ages. Then she said, 'Alright, Brian, but promise me that you will be careful and be back home before dark. I will make you some sandwiches and a drink'.

I think that I was quaking with excitement. I had a small rucksack in which I put my picnic. Walking to Walworth Road to get a bus, I really felt like a big boy. When I got there, I knew which direction I wanted to travel: towards London Bridge and the River. The first bus said, 'Imperial War Museum, Lambeth'. I thought, 'Brilliant', climbed upstairs, followed by a conductor, who just looked at me and went back down. About 20 minutes later, we were there. I got off the bus and gazed in awe at the big naval guns outside the building; however, walking up to the entrance doors, I saw they were shut.

There was a notice board saying, 'Open Daily, 11 a.m. to 5 p.m. Unattended children must be over 12 years old'. Realising that I was too young, I looked at my watch anyway. The one Dad had given to me when I had started my little business looking after bikes at Barking Football ground (when I was eight). It showed five to eleven. I decided to wait five minutes and take a peek inside.

Within one minute, noises came from within of bolts sliding, and the big doors started to move. I was the only one outside, my eyes wide open. Inside, two men in military uniforms were looking at me as they opened the doors. I noticed that one of them had an 'RASC' badge on his upper sleeve, and on his jacket breast was a small nameplate with his name, 'Joseph Andrew Thomas'.

I looked at it in amazement; they were my Dad's Christian names, and in WWII, he had been in the RASC. The man walked over to me saying, 'Are you alright, young man'? I told him that I was OK and explained the extreme coincidence. He was very interested and asked where my Dad had been (stationed) in WWII. I told him that Dad had been in charge of a vehicle repair and recovery unit based in Breda, Holland, in the latter part of the War. He lived there with a family who owned a soap factory with vehicle workshops and repaired Allied vehicles where necessary and possible. The family were very nice, and appreciative and would send Mum and I presents and letters. Joseph listened interestedly, then said, 'That's brilliant; what is your name, young man'?

'Brian, but my English teacher has just renamed me, Barnaby, after Barnaby Rudge, so call me that, please. He is a really lovely man called Mr. Barham - he has cast me in two plays recently, as Long John, in 'Robin Hood', and Shylock, in 'The Merchant of Venice'. I often see him in Barking Town Centre pushing his disabled daughter around in her wheelchair. He always calls out, "Hello, Barnaby. How are you today"?

'I am staying with my Auntie Eva in Walworth for a few days. She has let me come out on my own. I was hoping to look round your museum, and then go to the "Monument". But I now see that I am not allowed in the Museum on my own'. Joseph looked at his mate who was standing quite near and listening, winked at him, and said. 'Ian, this young man is too young to come in on his own, he has told me that he is dying for a piddle, so I am going to show him where it is. I might take him the long way round so he can see one or two of our Tanks, OK'? He winked again and took me in.

We walked in with me looking all round, in amazement. There was a big tank by the left-hand wall; Joseph noticed my eyes opening wide as I cried out, 'Is that a German tank'?

'Yes, it is. It's one of our best exhibits - a Panzer V - captured in Holland, by the way. It was in good condition; we painted out the German insignias, put ours on, and fitted an English transmitter. Within a few days, it was chasing the Huns'. Joseph was as good as

59

his word and took me past the best exhibits on the way to the toilets, returning to the exit a different way.

I thanked him very much and said to him that I would tell Dad all about it. As I walked out the doors, he saluted me. I cherish that memory to this day. I have taken my own children there at least twice, boring them each time by recounting that story.

Walking to the bus stop for my next destination, 'The Monument', I felt as though I was walking on air. The second bus to come along was the one I wanted. Once again, I sat upstairs; I don't know why, but the conductor didn't charge me this time, either.

Auntie Eva had done me two sarnies: one sliced boiled egg and tomato, the other cheese and tomato. Brilliant - I love tomatoes to this day. Especially since I found out that they are thought to have the highest antioxidant activity of all the carotenoids, and are rich in lycopene, which is particularly good for men in warding off prostate cancer. Anyway, no digressing. Back to the story.

I alighted at the Monument, and noticing the big seat at the base of it, I plonked myself down and ate one half of each sarnie. Something that I still do if I have two different filled rolls or sarnies. I can't seem to make my mind up about which I prefer; it won't surprise you to know that I have other peculiarities.

After eating, I had a swig of Auntie's drink, stood up and read the inscription on the tablet, and was fascinated to read all the facts then and since. Then, I walked round to the entrance; I think the charge was thruppence of which I had one. I realised that was the first time that day I had spent anything.

A group of people let me go ahead of them, and I manfully, for my age, set about tackling the 311 steps. I didn't struggle until about the last 300, haha, only joking. Eventually reaching the top, I first looked towards St. Paul's Cathedral, trying to imagine the spot where the fire had started. At my age, the whole experience was breathtaking, it was exciting going over London Bridge on the upper deck of the bus, but this was in a different league. Looking down at the River Thames, and river life stirred something in me.

I actually think that my love of boats started germinating that day. I have since sailed the full length of the Thames several times and had a boat on the upper Thames for five years. One of my prized photos shows me on a mobile phone with Tower Bridge close in the background. On a small, holding platform, with my old Scandinavian cruiser tied up beside me, waiting to 'lock in' at St. Katherines Dock.

That photo was taken at an opportune moment by my, metaphorically speaking, little brother Graham. We were en route to Twickenham to watch Martin Johnson's Rugby Testimonial. Looking back, I realise that, as well as loving Auntie Eva and other close family members, I have always loved 'Thamesis Fluvius'. It was fascinating to find out that Romans named it that after invading Britain. Now, now, Brian! No more digressing. It is so easy and tempting at my age.

Yes, looking down through the railings and security wires at ten years of age was awesome, wonderful, and brilliant! I checked my watch - oh no - time to climb down the many stairs and make my way back to my adorable Auntie Eva's. I managed to get the right buses and got back to Wooler Street, more or less on time.

Auntie was most impressed, although, I think due to worry, scolded me a bit; that was the first and last time ever. My little holiday came to an end, and Dad, Mum, and my two little brothers came to collect me.

On the way home, I couldn't stop talking about the good time that I had enjoyed. Dad was most impressed when I told him about the War Museum and Joseph Andrew Thomas. It really made him smile. I think that I fell asleep as we went through Rotherhithe Tunnel; this gave everyone's ears a rest.

Within days, I was engrossed with my mates, roller skating, roller hockey, and generally having fun. I don't know where the next few years went; they literally flew by. I finished senior school, and formed a company with Dad.

Then, I met Beryl, got married, and the children came along: Deborah, Andrew, and then Caroline. Afterwards, I bought a house in Seven Kings. I always kept in close contact with Auntie Eva, eventually taking my own children up to see her. They would have the obligatory 'killmequicks', and of course, lots of cuddles. Auntie was always her jovial self. Then, one day, when I was 28, and at our office in Barking, the phone rang.

At the time, Mum was ill in bed with a bad cold, and Dad had taken some sea fishermen out in our coach to Walmer in Kent. My phone rang, and on answering, it was my cousin Dennis phoning from work in Nottingham. His Mum, my Auntie Eva, had had a fall, and been rushed to St. Thomas Hospital in London. He said that she might possibly be in a coma.

To say that I was shocked to the core would be an understatement. I ran upstairs to tell Mum, and that I was going straight to St Thomas Hospital. I ran across the road to my old Rover 75, driving it at full pelt to the hospital. One hour and four minutes later, I parked up and sprinted to the Desk. Asking the whereabouts of Eva Gray, I was told she was in Room 8, on the second floor. I walked up very fast, and along the corridor. The fourth door on the right was open, and the name on the door tallied.

I walked in to see Auntie Eva half-sitting up in bed, eyes wide open, looking towards the door. I felt an enormous surge of relief. I rushed over to her with a big smile on my face, putting my arms around her. I said, 'Hello, Auntie. How are you'? There was no reply, no sign of recognition whatsoever.

My heart started racing; I waved a hand up and down in front of her eyes. Nothing at all. I was mortified, very frightened, with the most helpless feeling in the world. Involuntarily, I burst into tears; a nurse walking down the corridor came into the room but could give me no information whatsoever. I stayed there for ages feeling helpless and eventually walking back down to the Desk.

There I was told that they weren't sure what had caused the seizure. They advised that there was no point in me staying there, and to phone the next morning for an update. I drove home at a much slower pace, which was sensible as tears were still running down my face. I hardly slept that night. My phone rang the next morning at 8.00. It was my Mum, feeling better herself, but with the worst news. Eva passed away at 6.30 a.m.

I am now 82; her passing away still rates as the most devastated I have ever felt about someone's death. My Dad died at 64 years in

East Ham Memorial Hospital, having had heart problems for some time; so no surprise. My beloved Mum died at 84 years, weighing less than six stone, having fought Motor Neurone Disease (MND) for three years; once again, no surprise. She died on Friday, 13th January 1995.

My brother Graham has a video of her dancing with him on Christmas Day, 19 days before she died. Trust Mum to go on Friday the thirteenth. MND robbed her of her ability to speak, so for the last two years of her life, she carried a notepad and pen, writing words as she would have spoken them.

She even had them in hospital on her deathbed. When she was well, she could talk for England. I have her last words in print. Mum lives on in my mind and some of my other stories.

Chapter 8
Barking Abbey Grammar School

During my latter months at Manor School, all pupils had to sit an examination for selection of their next school - Grammar, Polytechnic, or Secondary. A couple of months later, the results came through. Well, you could have knocked me down with a feather: I had passed - and been selected to go to a top grade Grammar school! My Dad went round telling people that I must have 'bunged' the examiners, haha! As if you could.

I remember the day clearly when my 'pass' letter came through. The same day, a rival, local removal contractor had begrudgingly booked Dad's coach to take a party of children, including his son Leslie to go to London. It was for Leslie's birthday celebration. I said 'begrudgingly', as Leslie's Dad, Fred, and mine were always at loggerheads. This was mainly because my dad had served in the War, while Fred had dodged military duty. To make matters worse, Fred had also stolen some of my Dad's work.

The rival contractor had generously extended an invitation to me to join the children on the trip. It was generous since I had rarely, if ever, spoken to Leslie or met him. It was to take us to an exhibition on the South Bank, called 'The Festival of Britain', in 1951, which was to commemorate the 100th anniversary of 'The Great Exhibition, 1851', at Crystal Palace. Apparently, over 8 million people visited The South Bank in a five-month period that year.

There were many features there, including 'The Skylon', a 300-ft high metal structure, which was taken down the following year. Apparently, some of it was melted down and made into 'paper knives' and other limited edition paraphernalia.

Yes, somehow, I had passed my 11-plus examination and was going to start at a posh school after the summer holiday. Dad received a letter from the school stating certain requirements that needed to be met before my first day at school. I had to be measured for a very smart blazer with my 'house' badge on (Charterhouse).

Dad also had to buy a leather satchel, and camel hair artist brushes, with paint from a specialist art shop in Ilford. Writing about these items is strange; I can still literally smell the leather satchel. School start day came along, and I got on a bus, feeling conspicuous. I walked along to find a seat, and the first empty one was next to a boy with the same uniform on.

I sat down and introduced myself; his name was Ian Rose. Where I was quite tall for my age, Ian was small, and seemingly an introvert. I looked at his blazer badge and saw that he was also part of Charterhouse. On arrival at the stop for the school, we alighted and walked in together. The main entrance doors led into a magnificent entrance hall. The beautiful oak-panelled walls had lists on them in gold leaf of previous, illustrious pupils - some of whom had gone on to Oxford, or Cambridge Universities. The floor was antique parquet in a geometric pattern. The whole effect was breathtaking.

Soon, a lovely old pendulum wall clock began to strike nine. At the same time, a loud clanging bell rang out along the corridor, and all of the pupils started walking fast towards it, joined by Ian and myself.

Two pairs of large doors were open; on walking through them, we found ourselves in a large, well-lit hall. At the far end of the hall was a raised stage with two men on it. Both were wearing black university gowns and mortarboard caps. One of them was tall with a commanding demeanour, well-built, with a ruddy complexion; the other was short, slim and with an ingratiating look.

Once the pupils were inside the hall, and were quiet, the taller man who I took to be the headmaster, spoke, with a lovely timbre in his voice. 'Good Morning to you all. My name is Mr. Young. I'm your headmaster. Standing next to me is Mr. Phillips, your assistant headmaster. Welcome to our school; we meet here every morning sharp at 9.00. Now, please form an orderly queue to take a hymnbook from the cabinet on your left. Return to where you are standing, we will sing Hymn No. 62'.

You could tell that everyone was impressed and very pleased to be in this brilliant, scholastic environment. After the hymn, we were told to assemble in the four corners of the hall. Each corner had a coloured shield hanging up with the names of the four houses: Benedict, Citeaux, Clugny, and Charterhouse. We all followed the 'Old man's orders'. Our form teacher, Miss Williams, introduced herself and asked us all, to follow her. En route to our classroom, we walked around a gorgeous, Old World quadrangle, which was beautifully structured and maintained.

It was divided into four quarters by neat, narrow, york stone paths, and each quarter was covered by manicured, freshly mowed lawn. There was a very attractive antique stone birdbath, brimming with water, in the middle. The last classroom on the right, facing the quadrangle, was ours. On the opposite side of the quadrangle were laboratories, and the girl's Domestic Science room; it was like being on a different planet. Miss Williams led us into our classroom, saying, 'You may sit wherever you please'. That was when I caught the Welsh lilt in her voice. Ian and I took adjoining seats at the back of the classroom, and the room was soon full. With one empty seat at the front.

Miss Williams took her mortarboard off and, turning to address the class, spoke, 'Right, as I said, I am your form teacher, and, as well as that, I will be teaching you the French language each week'. There was a slight buzz of interest and excitement in the air, on hearing this. Next, we were all told to neatly empty our satchels onto our desks. This job, given our excitement, took quite a little while, with a discernible buzz in the air. After about 10 minutes, Miss said, 'Put your notebooks on your desks for our first lesson'.

I am not quite sure when or why I became the class 'clown', or if it happened that first day. I had never been of that mind or inclination at my two previous schools and can neither explain nor condone such stupid behaviour. However, that is exactly what happened quite early on during my time at Barking Abbey. I totally accept that it was very ignorant. I cannot offer any excuse, rhyme, or reason for it. Over time some of the class would laugh at my stupid behaviour, and I, even more stupidly, indulged more in it. In the early days, it was quite infrequent, but as the years went by, it happened more often.

Having said that, overall, I really enjoyed my time there. The front of the school was occupied with playing fields, where, in the summer, school sports competitions took place. I made some good friends there. At one end of the school was the music hall. The music teacher, Mr. Miller, was fixated on Edvard Greig's music, and 'Peer Gynt', nursing his dying mother, was played to us repeatedly. Not surprisingly, hearing it 67 years later still stirs me.

The other end of the school was the art studio, run by Miss Buckingham. She was quite tall, with long, straggly blonde dyed hair; her facial makeup consisted of excessive use of bright red lipstick, with clown-like white daubing on her cheeks, which were heavily lined. Her nickname? Bucketface! She had, presumably, at some time, really pissed someone off.

Two very strange things happened during my time there. Once, while there were several of us on the sports field, she came out of a door at the side of her studio, and a javelin came hurtling through the air, narrowly missing her. Neither myself nor my friends saw anyone nearby who may have thrown it. The police were called but could not solve the mystery of who or why anyone had done it.

On another occasion, we were in our classroom when a couple of policemen, accompanied by two ambulance men pushing a patient's trolley, came rushing past our door on their way to Bucketface's artroom. Minutes later, they returned with an even whiter than usual Bucketface on it. She was off school for several days. Apparently, someone had tried to poison her with some substance in her coffee. No one was ever charged over either offence.

The row of laboratories across the quadrangle included a woodwork room, the teacher there was Mr. W.I.M. Petty. As you have observed, this spells Wimp. Whether that had any effect whatsoever on his personality, God knows. But, as a teacher, he was a bully. He was a bit below average height and very wiry with a 'pushy' personality. He drove an old 'Morris minor', to and from school each day. Absolutely none of his pupils liked him.

One day, when we were in Year 3, he was absent from school; now, this was a rare occurrence. He didn't turn up for school for the next three days. Now, it was a known fact that Mr. Miller, the music teacher ,didn't like him. During a music lesson at the end of that week, I noticed that Mr. Miller had a smirk on his face. I couldn't resist asking him if he knew why Mr. Petty was off school. Well, the smirk turned into a broad smile. 'Come close', he said to me and my best friend, Tony Young, 'And don't tell anyone what I am about to disclose. Petty lived just outside Brentwood; his wife was an invalid and housebound. Petty would go out shopping in Brentwood alone in the Morris minor, wearing his wife's clothes, even her knickers. The other day, he reversed into an old lady in a car park, knocking her over. The police were called, and he was taken into custody, and charged with driving without due care and attention. And also crossdressing'.

Tony and I almost wet ourselves laughing; we told everyone we met inside and outside school. Wimp did actually come back to work as a teacher at Barking Abbey, but after a couple of months, resigned. I think that it was his bullying attitude, combined with the looks and nods of the pupils, that made him throw in the towel.

Unfortunately, I was stupid enough to play the class clown, too often. I know it was ridiculous. Mr. Young was our mathematics teacher, and I can remember on one occasion, he called my name out, saying, 'This is a red letter day for you today, Rudge. You have got 10 out of 10 for the math's question paper I gave you'. This was definitely NOT, the norm. I was increasingly upsetting the Old Man and being told to go to his office for a 'Whacking'. This meant the cane and my making my way along one of the two quadrangles to the Old Man's office. It was a very large room, with two imposing desks; the slightly smaller desk was Mr. Phillips, and the larger one was the Old Man's.

There were two large bookcases and two large G Plan fireside chairs. By now, I knew the procedure very well: Knock twice loudly on the door, and listen out for a gruff, 'Enter'. On entering the room, Mr. Phillips, looking flustered, would be at his desk in the left-hand corner. By law, he had to be there as a witness of fair play. The Old Man would usher you towards the centre of the office, where the fireside chairs were.

He always had an extra-red face as he grabbed at one of the

chairs, pulling it to one side so he could get a good swing at you with his cane, the veins on his forehead really standing out. He would then take the fitted cushion off the chair whilst barking at you, 'Bend over and hold the front rack of the chair!' At this point, I would say, 'Sorry, sir, can you show me how? I have forgotten exactly how you mean'.

Now, this wasn't an act of bravado. I don't actually know why I said it, but I did. The reaction from the Headmaster, and Mr. Phillips, was instant: the latter would look even more flustered and uneasy, and the Old Man visibly shook with anger.

He would bend forward, gritting his teeth, his veins looking as though they might burst, and grab the front rack of the chair, causing the chair to move closer to him. As he stood up, I would say, 'Of course, I remember now'. Then, taking the same posture as he had, Whack!

The first swipe struck, followed by five more. I always stayed in that position for a good few seconds before saying, 'Have you finished, Sir'?

'Yes, get up'! The Old Man growled. 'Am I free to go now, Sir'?

'Yes, get out of here'! As I opened the door to leave, I would look over at Mr. Phillips and nod; he would not acknowledge me, and I would walk off to my classroom. Writing the last script caused me to cringe with embarrassment.

How could I have been so ignorant, pigheaded, and crass! Maybe it has been cathartic, to me, to write this. The only answer I can give is: I don't know. I just cannot explain my attitude. I am a sensitive, caring person; however, on reflection, it was as if I had a demon in my brain during those school years.

It got worse each year, unfortunately. A few days before our summer break, there was a 'Parents Open Day'. This was to show our parents how we had progressed in the year. The school was cleaned thoroughly, lawns neatly mowed, and flower gardens arranged beautifully, for this event.

Everything was made to look spick-and-span. The laboratories were open and showing woodwork, and metalwork creations, on show. The Domestic Science room was made to look like an upmarket French Pattisserie, with delicious pastries and cakes on show.

Now, what I am going to disclose next sorely bugs me to this day – I honestly don't know how it started. I had what you would term 'hangers on', people who were always around me, laughing at my jokes, etc., and generally hanging around, and often egging me on. We were in the Dom-sci Room, as we called it, just my cronies and myself. Someone suggested eating one of the pastries on display. One of us took the absolutely crazy decision to do it. Kerpow! It happened. The rest stood transfixed for a very few seconds, then someone else decided to do the same. Absolutely insane and stupid! Within no time, it became a feeding frenzy – a bit like you may see animals at the zoo – when the keeper throws the food. Now, it may have been me who started it, but I honestly don't remember.

What seemed like seconds later, the whole display had vanished, with just crumbs and pastry flakes left on the plates. The idiot perpetrators, myself included, just quickly walked away. We all made our back to our classroom, and sat down.

I think everyone felt aghast (I certainly did). Writing this, a lifetime later, a term once used by disgraced U.S. President Nixon comes to mind, 'You can't put the toothpaste back in the tube'. Within a very short time, a red-faced Headmaster came storming towards our classroom, his robe billowing behind him. He marched up to my desk and yanked me up to a standing position, yelling, 'My Study, Now'!

I limply followed him, expecting the worst whacking of my life. On arrival at his study, he didn't, as I was expecting, start moving the chairs about in anger. No, that didn't happen; instead, he motioned me to sit on one. I did as asked, and he started speaking, 'I know that you must have been involved in the debacle in the Domestic Science Room. I am giving you two choices, either you stay down a year, or you leave the school today'.

I must have considered the options, but I don't remember doing so. I replied, 'I will leave now, Sir'.

I walked, for the last time ever, along the quadrangle to collect my satchel and books and walked away from the school. I know that

I had been an absolute idiot. As I walked along the road towards the bus stop for home, I saw, in the distance, a removal lorry that I recognised.

I walked along toward it. My Dad and Uncle John were unloading it, I took my blazer off and started to help them. Thus, starting my life in house, office, and machinery removals.

It has kept me fit and served me well. Maybe it is my strange, even warped outlook, but I am glad for what I have done for a living. I have travelled the U.K. and Europe extensively met with lots of adventures, done lots of daily cardiovascular exercises, and can tell lots of stories. Had my Dad been involved with a sedentary, boring business, I could have easily followed him and died a young, unfit man.

Chapter 9
Chelmsford Prison Fish

Around springtime 1954, my Dad had a removal lorry, and acquired a 27-seater Bedford duple coach in which he used to take workmen, early mornings, to work in Barking, Essex, Power station, picking them up after work and dropping them at Barking town centre. Occasionally, mostly on Saturdays, but sometimes during the week, he would take theatre-goers to London's West end. When that happened (I was fourteen at the time), Uncle John (who worked for Dad) and I, would have to thoroughly clean the coach, including every window inside and out.

As I've mentioned earlier, he wasn't my real Uncle. John had met my Dad during the War, and they had become good friends; he came to live with us and work for Dad after the War. Doing household removals and, more recently, driving the coach. The coach had two other users, both angling clubs, one group was fresh water, and the other, sea anglers. The freshwater anglers called themselves 'Becmain'; they all worked for Briggs Motor Bodies at Dagenham making motor bodies for Fords, both cars and vans.

They had been looking out for a lake of their own for some time. One had recently come along, and they bought the lease for it, along with two acres of land. This was in Childerditch Lane, near Brentwood, Essex, U.K. There was, however, a problem: the lake was seriously understocked with fish. Bill Hurley, the club's founder (a very nice man with a great sense of humour), had a brother-in-law named Rodney Brown. Rodney was like the archetypal Prison Governor - which is what he actually was. Of Chelmsford Prison.

Where Bill was naturally funny, Rodney was naturally very serious, with a face like a baboon's arse. During a phone call, Bill told Rodney of the lake situation, who said, 'Leave it with me. I have an idea'. A few days later, Rodney phoned Bill and said, 'I have spoken to the Prison Board of Governors and raised the situation of the lake within the prison grounds'. Now, it turned out that some of the Board had been 'angling', excuse the pun, for some time, to have the lake - which was a considerable size - removed.

The prison was being enlarged and would need a bigger exercise yard. Now, the fact was that their lake was extremely overstocked with fish, and the Board reasoned that it would be a step in the right direction to start dissipating the fish. At an extraordinary general meeting, the Board passed a motion to allow events to take place related to the clearance of the lake. Better still, a resolution was passed to allow a civilian vehicle to enter the prison grounds, under supervision, to begin the process.

This had to take place very early on a Sunday morning, such that the work was finished and the vehicle and any helpers gone from the grounds by 10 a.m. Bill met my Dad, and they hatched a plan: go to Briggs Bodies on Saturday with the lorry, and collect two clean metal tanks, 4 ft high and 5 ft square. They also required: an adapted device, made by the Briggs company's electrical laboratory, that used submersible electrodes to stun the fish, a small portable ex-military generator, an electric water pump, 20 ft of large bore rubber hose, two large nets on poles and four large metal buckets.

I went with Uncle John in the lorry to collect the equipment and was absolutely fascinated by it all. I was most pleased when Dad told me that I could go on the lorry, with him driving, the next day. Mum made us lots of sandwiches and two flasks of tea. We set off from our yard, just across the road from the house, sharp at five the next morning. Mum was outside our front door waving with one hand and holding Patsy, our cocker spaniel with the other. My two little brothers were still asleep.

We got to Chelmsford prison about an hour later, and four members of the Becmain Angling Club met us there. Rodney, and two prison staff opened the entrance gates, and we pulled up as close as possible to the oval lake. There was a low wall round it with a gap about six feet across, five steps down to water level, and a large rowing boat bobbing about. Bill Hurley was delegating jobs to his fellow club members.

My Dad, who had been in charge of a transport troop in the War, started affixing the rubber hose to the water pump and generator. He put approximately 2 ft depth of water into each tank. Bill wanted to row out on the lake to assess the situation. By now, Dad had put the desired amount of water from the lake into the tanks. Bill rowed back to the steps to put the equipment in the dinghy. The equipment comprised the electrodes, generator, two nets, and two buckets.

After putting everything on board, plus himself and Jim (the club secretary), he still wanted one more to make everything go as smoothly and quickly as possible. Especially bearing in mind our deadline to pull out of the prison. But there was precious little room on the boat. Suddenly he called out, 'Barnaby! Come and jump in! Quickly'? I didn't need telling twice; elated, I jumped in and out we rowed; within a few strokes, we could see several fish. Jim had already assembled everything, fired up the generator after affixing the electrodes, and dropped them over the stern into the water. Almost immediately, a dozen fish were floating on the surface. Luckily, Jim had also 'three quarter' filled the buckets.

Bill shouted at Jim and me, 'Scoop those fish up as quick as you can'! We did, popping them straight into the buckets. Within 10 minutes, the buckets were brimming with fish, the early morning sun showing their glistening brilliant silver shades. Bill then rowed ashore, and strong hands grabbed the buckets, gently pouring the contents into the storage tanks with the same temperature water in them.

This process was repeated many times until looking into the tanks, you could barely see the bottom for fish. Bill went ashore to double-check the tanks and came out of the lorry clapping his hands, shouting, 'Fantastic, boys! Let's start packing up'!

Rodney came onto the back of the lorry, had a look in the tanks, and pulled a very rare smile, saying, 'Brilliant effort, chaps! Put your equipment in the lorry. I'll see you out of the gate ahead of time. Thanks'!

Dad had poured us a tea each and opened the sarnies Mum had made for us. Bread and dripping with slices of her homemade brawn, with thick mustard on them, mine and Dad's favourite. Dad then drove us as slowly as possible - so the water in the tanks didn't swoosh about too much - to Childerditch and the lake. Bill and his fishing colleagues closely followed us. Dad said that was to check that we weren't driving too fast and further upsetting the fish.

On arrival at Childerditch, it was all hands on deck. We gently got the fish out, using the nets and four buckets this time. Bill was amazed: not one fish had been injured. He calculated that we had safely transferred over 1,000 fish. He also said the lake was 60 ft deep and 200 ft across. Then, he said to me, 'Thanks very much'! And that if I wanted to "join the club and fish" there, I could do so as an honorary member, at no charge'.

I said, 'Thanks for the offer, but not at the moment'. It was just as well. I found out, as the years rolled by, I must be the world's worst fisherman. However, the pleasure I had in the dinghy has, I am sure, given me a lifelong love of boats. I have owned several and had many adventures in them. Looking back to that day, it also probably rates as my best day out with Dad ever.

Printed in Great Britain
by Amazon